PRAISE for *THE*

When two compassionate minds come together the love that Jesus demonstrated for the hurting masses is clearly visible and a well balanced approach to ministry is the result. The combination of Fran Jones and Dr. John McCoy takes the work of the modern deaconess to another, more splendid level. Their work is superb and reflects deep spiritual insight. This publication is a "must read" for pastors and lay church leadership alike.

Reverend Dr. Morris L. Shearin
President, Baptist Convention of the District of Columbia
Pastor, Israel Baptist Church, Washington, DC

The work that Fran Jones has done to empower deaconesses in the churches of our nation is second to none. This publication is just another sterling example of the excellence in ministry to which Fran Jones ascends and excels.

Reverend Dr. Patrick J. Walker
President, Ministers' Conference of Washington, DC and Vicinity
Pastor, The New Macedonia Baptist Church, Washington, DC

Solid, Sound, Substantive... Once again, Fran Jones has produced a work that will bless the body of Christ. I wholeheartedly, enthusiastically endorse and recommend this book. Fran has used these principles to bless not only our church in Denver but many other churches throughout this country and beyond. If you are looking to improve leadership in your local church, then this blessed work is a must read! I congratulate Fran Jones on her latest effort to get us to the next level of leadership in our churches.

Dr. Terence E. Hendricks
Pastor, King Baptist Church, Denver, Colorado

Fran Jones shows us that the urban challenge for the 21st century deaconess is to change our ministry to meet the current social culture. Having read all of Fran Jones' books and attended her workshops, classes, and conferences from DC to Denver, I can assure you this book will surpass all expectations.

Leslie B. Turner
Deaconess, Fort Foote Baptist Church, Ft. Washington, MD

THE 21st CENTURY DEACONESS

MEETING THE URBAN CHALLENGE

Fran A. Jones
John L. McCoy, D. Min.

Highly Favored Publishing™
Bowie, Maryland

The 21st Century Deaconess: Meeting the Urban Challenge
Copyright © 2011 Fran A. Jones and John L. McCoy

Cover photo © iStockphoto

Published by Highly Favored Publishing™
3540 Crain Highway #440
Bowie MD 20716 USA
(301) 257-6659
highlyfavoredpublishing@gmail.com
www.highlyfavoredpublishing.com
Highly Favored Publishing™ is an entity of Highly Favored, L.L.C.

First Printing, 2011

Printed in the United States of America

ISBN 978-0-9835157-2-2

Library of Congress Control Number: 2011912228

No part of this publication may be reproduced, stored in a retrieval system, or transmitted, in any form, or by any means, electronic, mechanical, photocopying, recording, or otherwise, without the prior consent of the publisher.

All scripture quotations, unless otherwise noted, are taken from the King James Version of the Holy Bible.

*This book is dedicated to the memory of our beloved
Sandra Yvette Mitchell.
Love for you remains forever in our hearts.*

ACKNOWLEDGEMENTS

A special appreciation to all the wonderful people who made this work possible. First and foremost, I give praises to my Savior and Lord, Jesus Christ.

To my husband, Earnest, you are the wind beneath my wings. I thank God for sending me you. So much of what I do could not be done without a man like you by my side. You are a man of few words, but your strength encourages me in many ways. I'm glad I have you to lean on and am so grateful to have you in my life. I Love You.

I extend my sincere appreciation and gratitude to Theresa McCoy, my sister. Where would I be without you in my life? Thank you for the many hours you spent assuring that this book would come to fruition. You are the "real" author. We are friends by divine providence and sisters by choice. Love Always!

To my precious daughter, Tina, and son, Jerome; you have always been a source of tremendous joy. I pray that this book will be an inspiration to the two of you. Know that through Christ you can accomplish anything.

To the giant of a man that I call friend and pastor, Rev. Dr. John L. McCoy, thank you for sharing your gift with me as co-author of this book. Only God knew that when we became friends, you would become my "contact" person. To God be the glory!

I would like to thank my wonderful family at The Word of God Baptist Church. Thank you for embracing me and showing me the agape kind of love.

To my six beautiful grandchildren, Anaiah, Kamau, Dikembwe, Arikah, Anele, and Kyra, I thank God for your love. I pray that my life has been an example for you, as I follow Christ. I love you with all my heart.

I would like to thank Melvette Melvin Davis, the outstanding publisher and editor of Highly Favored Publishing, for the superb preparation of the manuscript for this project and turning it into a meticulous work of quality that superseded my imagination. Thank you for all the encouragement throughout the journey.

Fran A. Jones

CONTENTS

FOREWORD
9

INTRODUCTION
MEETING THE URBAN CHALLENGE
12

CHAPTER ONE
A DEACONESS BIRTHED BY PAIN
23

CHAPTER TWO
MEETING THE URBAN CHALLENGE:
THE NEED FOR STREET-WISE DEACONESSES
40

CHAPTER THREE
MEETING THE URBAN CHALLENGE:
NOT FOR DEACONESSES ONLY
47

CHAPTER FOUR
MEETING THE URBAN CHALLENGE:
ORPHANED GIRLS LIVING WITH BOTH PARENTS
57

CHAPTER FIVE
Meeting the Urban Challenge: The Calling of Deaconesses
65

CHAPTER SIX
Meeting the Urban Challenge: The Power of the Tongue
76

CHAPTER SEVEN
Meeting the Urban Challenge: Scary Stalkers and Safe Houses
82

CHAPTER EIGHT
Meeting the Urban Challenge: The Church, a Place Where Miracles Happen
87

CHAPTER NINE
Meeting the Urban Challenge: The Young Women Most at Risk
97

AFTERWORD
112

NOTES
115

FOREWORD
Pastor John L. McCoy, D. Min.

Many have attempted to convey the long-term effects of the absence of a father in the life of a woman. However, one only needs to examine the life of Fran Jones to get an idea of the damaging consequences of such an absence, which are often preceded by sudden abandonment. The trauma of waking up one morning and finding that your daddy who promised never to leave you is gone becomes a watershed moment that often damns a daughter to a dungeon of darkness much worse than divorce.

As Fran's Pastor, she has shared with me the "post-abandonment" period of her life. Her father, as seen through the eyes of his little girl, not only divorced her mother, but divorced her, as well. When he left, he left and never returned. Her most vivid memory of his absence is on her sixteenth birthday. She was so sure that he would, at some time during her celebration, appear and dance with his daughter, for his daughter's sake. After all, she was his "precious baby," "the apple of [his] eye," and "the light of [his] life," to use his words. At the time, it was not difficult for her to envision her knight in shining armor, bearing merely the gift of his presence, appearing at some point at her party and asking, "May I have this dance?" She waited and hoped until, at last, her hope seemed to wane as the evening turned into the last dance and no daddy. No one knew her

Cinderella-like expectations. No one knew that his failure to appear would leave such an indelible mark. From that moment on, the scarlet letter "R" for "Rejected" would stigmatize her well into the fifth decade of her life. Fran cried that night for what seemed like 10,000 nights. In the darkness, she searched for answers that would never come. How could he be anywhere but his daughter's sixteenth, seventeenth, eighteenth, twenty-first, fortieth, and fiftieth birthday celebrations? What would keep a father from fulfilling the longings of a daughter who lived in the same city and sending a card that read, "Thinking of you" or "Congratulations on your high school graduation?" Or, maybe just a simple card for a depressed daughter who had not truly smiled since she woke up one morning and discovered her daddy gone. How can a father leave a daughter to the predatory habits of street-wise men and not desire to protect her? Such unanswered questions can cause the most beautiful woman to see blemishes on her body that are not visible. Such unanswered questions can cause a woman to hear voices of rejection that were never spoken. Such unanswered questions can bring a veil of darkness into a woman's life that even the light of the gospel will have difficulty penetrating.

In this text, Fran shares the effects of the absence and abandonment of her father and admits a pain so deep that even the powerful hand of God has had difficulty healing. There is no doubt in my mind that absence and abandonment by fathers causes daughters a sense of loneliness, worthlessness, and anger that can only result in one failed relationship with men after another. There is little wonder why the subsequent opposite-sex relationships in the life of Frances Moore were destined to fail. Frances Moore carried within her bosom a hopelessness that becoming Fran Jones could not eradicate. Pain is a by-product of wounds left unattended. Pain is the fate of any relationship that

FOREWORD

hinges on one party's dependence on the validation of another. Pain is the magnet that draws wounded people to other wounded people and becomes the devil that dogs and damns them both. Deaconess Fran Jones has cautioned young "Frances Moores" in seminars across this country to "wait until you are healed from the wounds of the past if you want a relationship that lasts. Without such healing, one merely moves from one degree of pain to another." Without the necessary emotional, psychological, and spiritual healing that brings about an emotional wholeness, one will wander from one toxic relationship to another, looking for love in all the wrong places. Without the necessary healing, a vast majority of women have become bitter, cynical, verbally abusive, and even violent. The lack of such healing will eventually, beyond a shadow of doubt, affect a woman's physical health.

In this book, Fran and I seek to share the benefits of the struggle we have shared as church officers over the past 25 years. It is our friendship of over 30 years, however, that has bonded us in a great struggle to save the life of "our" daughter. Our friendship has witnessed the struggle of our daughter's pervasive drug addiction. Fran's daughter, the young woman for whom I had been a father figure for over two decades, was brutally murdered over four years ago—the circumstances are still unknown, and perpetrator is still at large. It is, therefore, in retrospect that we review the issues that perhaps led to her murder in hope of preventing the murder of many other daughters who leave small, Southern towns for the promises of the big cities in America.

INTRODUCTION
MEETING THE URBAN CHALLENGE

"Disciplining urban populations is perhaps the most urgent task confronting the church."[1]

Pastor McCoy

I do not believe there has ever been a time when the work of the deaconess has been more needed than in the dawning decades of this 21st century, and there has never been a place where the work of the deaconess is more vital than in urban America. Since what historians call the "Second Great Migration," African Americans born in rural, Southern towns have believed there was a "promised land" up North. Tired of the inequities of the South and the economic treadmill of share cropping and driven by a vision of land flowing with "milk and honey" opportunities, post-World War II African American men heeded the cries of "Go North, young man; go North, and make your fortune." In post-World War II America, many African American servicemen, after serving tours of duty overseas, decided not to return to their Southern roots. A popular post-World War I song, "How Ya Gonna Keep 'Em Down On the Farm After They've Seen Paree,"[2] also describes the mood of the post-World War II era as relates to a broader exposure to the urban world for both blacks and whites. The degradation of signs that read "For Whites Only" did nothing to dim the glitter of Northern lights, and it was with the ravages of the Great

INTRODUCTION

Depression in mind that African Americans saw in Northern cities opportunities to realize the American Dream. Letters, postcards, and photographs mailed from cities like New York, Chicago, Washington, DC, and Philadelphia created excitement in men who had only known plowing Southern fields and picking Southern cotton. The lure of respectability and the luxury of not having to say "Yes, Sir" and "No, Ma'am" were attractive to people who had never been called "Mr." or "Mrs."

First, the men came, with married men making promises of sending for their wives and children. My father was one of them. My mother conveyed to me how he promised that as soon as he got a job and got settled, he would send for us. Well, apparently he never got "settled," for I have personally never laid eyes on him. He seemed to have disappeared into the smog of the Northern lights. The McCoy family was not alone, as much of the South was drained of its young men. The economic toll on Southern African American families, especially the "wives in waiting," was enormous. The young men who decided to stay put literally ran rampant through the women who were left behind. Southern farming communities were so inundated with "bastard babies" that "sowing one's wild oats" became a rite of passage to manhood for Southern, African American men. The baby boom was in full force in the South in the mid-1940s. It was into such a social climate that my generation entered the world.

Eventually, young, African American women began to imagine the possibilities of life beyond the humiliation of having babies and the stigma that even the church attached to unmarried women who were in the "family way." To avoid such humiliation, many soon-to-be grandfathers sent their daughters to family members living in other cities to give birth, and these daughters returned with a child who was passed off as a cousin, nephew, or niece. There were many children raised in households who honestly thought their mother was their cousin or aunt, only to learn later that their cousin or aunt was, in reality, their mother. To escape the clutches of such a scenario, the answer for many young, African American women born or raised in the South became apparent—at least in their eyes. Again, it was, "Go North!" This migration trend continues even today.

Driven to cities like never before, young women today are facing issues they have never before encountered or imagined. Forced to navigate the multi-cultured, ethnically-diverse, tension- and stress-filled, concrete-paved "jungles" of Northern cities like New York, Newark, Chicago, Philadelphia, and Washington, DC, unsuspecting young women are often overwhelmed with the challenge of navigating city life and city folks. As they arrive at big-city bus depots and train stations, they are often easily recognizable, and in many cases, they become easy prey to pimps and other people who seek to exploit their naiveté. The need for a safe haven—a friendly face, adopted mothers and big sisters, spiritual direction, and guidance through the maze and madness of city life—is absolutely essential. Without such support, the city becomes a mean place that chews women up and spits them out. It is for this reason that I believe the battle for the souls of young, African American women, and all the beautiful, starry-eyed, young black girls who now sing in the Sunbeam choirs of our churches, will prove to be most challenging in the inner cities of America.

"Moore" Pain and Double Trouble

In Paul L. Dunbar's poem "Life,"[3] he describes life for African Americans as "A crust of bread and a corner to sleep in / A

INTRODUCTION

minute to smile and an hour to weep in / A pint of joy to a peck of trouble / And never a laugh but the moans come double." This poem perfectly describes the life of Frances Moore in 1964.

In 1964, Frances Moore was a young, African American woman with *more pain* than she could handle and *double trouble* with two young girls born out of wedlock. Like many young women of the time, she boarded a train heading for the concrete jungle of the big city, looking for a fresh start. She arrived at Union Station in Washington, DC with exactly $24 to her name, 3 tattered suitcases, and 2 little girls. She had previously thought downtown Charlotte was a big city, but amid the honking horns of taxi cabs, the screeching of street car wheels, the busyness of people rushing from one place to another, the shouting of people selling newspapers, and the wailing of sirens, the nation's capital was Charlotte to the tenth power. If you didn't move fast enough, you were pushed aside; if you didn't know where you were going, you were afraid to ask directions. The landscape was a maze of tall buildings and statues. She was overwhelmed by the challenges of such an environment. The city seemed so filled with peril and deception. The very ambiance of this powerful, impersonal city was unlike anything she had ever known. No one spoke to anyone. People were not people, just numbers. A young woman walking down the street was inundated with flirtatious solicitations of "Hey, Mama" or "Where ya going, Baby?" It seemed as if those who paid any attention to her wanted something from her. She noticed that seldom did men look into a woman's eyes, but they seemed to be always searching for something in her blouse or under her skirt. Encounters with men were always uncomfortable, for it seemed as if men were always sizing up something behind a woman.

Frances was most afraid for her daughters. Her concern from the moment she stepped off the train in Washington, her primary focus, was always their safety. It was always, "Sandra, hold Tina's hand." "Tina, come over here." "Don't touch that." "Sit here 'til I come back!" "Sandra, where's your sister?" "You all stay close to Mama." The attention of Frances in this big city was always divided between what she was trying to do and her little girls. This did not change for the next 20 years. Yet, with all her vigilance, a predator was able to quietly penetrate her protective hedge. This predator was a drug dealer. For that, it has always been difficult for Fran not to blame herself.

Plenty of Blame to Go Around

After 15 years of living in the city, the eldest daughter of Frances, Sandra, began to experiment with drugs. Eventually, she became addicted. The next 20 years became a blur, an endless montage of treatment programs and relapses, frustration and anger, accusations and recrimination. It seemed that all Fran could really do was sit in the dark theater of parenthood and view the slow, torturous decline. The drama was as an endless soap opera—as the world turned. Frances and her daughter Sandra seemed to be in a constant search for tomorrow as the guiding light of God's Word seemed to be the only real hope. Frances hung onto that hope as if it were a rope; in truth, it was. As the pastor of both Frances and Sandra, I spent an estimated quarter of my pastorate focused on Sandra and her "issue." I viewed firsthand the devastation of a life in the constant grip of addiction. To Sandra's credit, she fought continually and courageously but, too often, alone.

Her mother bore most of the blame and, therefore, most of the burden. One only needs to be placed in such a predicament to know just how little help is available to assist in such a struggle. Therefore, there is enough blame to go around. One could blame the grandfather, who abandoned Sandra's mother, for pushing the domino that began the chain of events that led to Sandra's addiction. One could place blame upon the father who was never in Sandra's life. One could blame the system that provided no real support for people addicted to drugs who were without the financial means of the rich and famous. This book, however, is not meant to place blame but to seek out answers that will aid the millions of young girls growing up in the cities of America who are at risk. For the city of bright lights and bustling traffic are danger zones and dark dungeons of horror where ferocious predators await the endless parade of Frances Moores and their daughters.

The Last Line of Defense
"And ye shall be witnesses, in Jerusalem, Judaea, and in Samaria" (Acts 1:8a)

Where can a parent turn when her child is on a road that has only two possible ends, the penitentiary or the cemetery? To whom should a parent look while trying to raise young children and at the same time attempting to scratch out a living in one of our nation's inner cities? What is the last line of defense for a single mother with young children in a big city? How can she protect them from the predatory practices of the pimps and pushers who lurk around most schools and playgrounds in the inner city? How do committed parents guard their children from cyber pedophiles who surf the web 24 hours a day for lonely young women, especially, to victimize? Jesus loves the little children. He encourages us to "allow the little children to come unto me, and forbid them not" (Mark 10:14). I contend that the absolute last line of defense for the children that Jesus so cherishes is churches in the inner city. As a pastor of a church in the inner city, I have presided at too many funerals for young people whose lives were snuffed out unnecessarily. As a pastor, I also have driven through the streets and witnessed too many young women in halter-tops and micro-mini skirts seeking the attention that should come from fathers early in their lives. I shall never forget something that Sandra said to me in one of our counseling sessions. She considered me her adopted father. One day, she looked to me and said, "Pastor, as my Dad, you are the only man in my life who has not tried to get into my underwear." What a frightening thought. What a sad commentary on the morality of men in America. What an indictment on our society. It was probably not an entirely true statement, but it certainly reflected the reality that there are too many men in positions to protect young women who, in the final analysis, end up preying upon them. The church is the last line of defense for young women like Sandra, but if the church does not live up to the admonition of Jesus to protect the daughters of Zion, it will cease to be relevant in the 21st century. And if the church continues to harbor men who *prey on* instead of *pray for* our young women, then it will, beyond a doubt, suffer the wrath of Almighty God. The time has come for the church to be the church; if not, it will burn in the eternal fires of hell along with those who victimize the vulnerable daughters of God.

Dealing with the Big Three
"Upon this rock I will build my church; and the gates of hell shall not prevail against it." Matthew 16:16b

As a pastor, I am well aware that churches are inundated with so many problems that it is overwhelming. When it comes to addressing issues related to young women's ministry, the church is faced with three obvious barriers. I call them "The Big Three." When Jesus spoke of the power of this organism called the church, He promised that the very "gates of hell shall not prevail against it" (Matthew 16:16b). Well, there are three very strong gates that must be dealt with if the church is going to be effective in ministering to young women: Financing, Blending, and Pastoral Trust.

1. **Financing**: The challenge of financing, alone, commands a great portion of a church's focus. Without adequate financing, a church's hands are hindered in many areas. If a church does not have adequate financial resources, it cannot provide the training necessary to equip deaconesses and other support staff to minister to young women. Additionally, churches need financial resources to provide space, equipment, and literature to reach young women not only within the walls of the church, but also within the community of the church.

2. **Blending**: In addition to the issue of financing, there is the challenge of blending different personalities into a unified group to work together for the common good. The stress associated with such blending has caused many pastors to develop ulcers and other stress-related physical ailments. Pastors especially face the challenge of how to convince hurting and angry African American men and women to work together when there are so many issues that separate them, how to get the young and the elderly to work together when their languages and viewpoints are often very different, and how to get families from varied socio-economic backgrounds to work in harmony with each other when issues of insecurity, envy, education, and economics make one family suspect of the other.

3. **Pastoral Trust**: In many churches, there is also the issue of distrust. Since the mid-80s, "tell-all" talk shows have exposed the sins and personal flaws of politicians, Catholic

priests, and evangelical pastors and preachers. Politicians have traditionally been objects of distrust, but in the African American community, the pastor/preacher has always held a sacred position of honor and respect. Such is no longer the case. Sadly, the most difficult challenge of pastors in the inner city is that of gaining the trust of the church's leadership and congregants. At a time when pastors ought to be able to work closely with various members of the church, pastors are forced to keep a safe distance for fear of some accusation that destroys their reputation or credibility. The greatest fear of most pastors in the sue-crazed environment of the inner city is to be caught alone with any female who walks into their studies. Panic sets in, as she could claim that he said something or touched her somewhere. It is her word against his, and he will come out the loser almost every time. Even if a jury of 10 million Mother Teresas clears him, the general consensus will be, "He got off." Thereafter, he will forever have to live with people, wherever he goes, pointing their fingers and whispering, "He is the one. Ain't that a shame! That's why I don't go to church." Surely, the seven most comforting words that fell from the lips of Christ that caring and dedicated pastors must rely upon are, *"The gates of hell shall not prevail."* Without this assurance, to pastor is to place oneself under too great a risk.

> *The time has come for the church to be the church; if not, it will burn in the eternal fires of hell along with those who victimize the vulnerable daughters of God.*

INTRODUCTION

There are many other issues and hindrances that distract churches and distort their focus on evangelizing, protecting, and ministering to young women in the dangerous, cold, impersonal, and predatory streets of the inner cities. However, churches must not allow themselves to be distracted or deterred from their divine duty. Young women must become a major priority of our churches. However, because of the aforementioned "Big Three" challenges, financing, blending, and pastoral trust, this priority primarily rests upon the female leaders of the church. Deaconesses must emerge as a major ministry force in the area of young women. No one is in more danger on the streets of the inner cities of this country than young women. This is my contention because they bear triple incentives for predators: physical weakness, sexuality, and an innate desire for male affection. Physical weakness allows young women to be overpowered physically. Sexuality makes young women vulnerable to men seeking to satisfy their own baser desires or seeking an income generating entity (prostitution, pornography, etc.). Innate desire for male affection often makes young women willing participants in their own exploitation. There is a saying, "An ounce of prevention is worth more than a pound of cure." Our churches must become proactive, and our greatest challenge is to reach young women before the pedophiles, pornographers, pimps, cyber predators, and angry, sadistic abusers reach them. It is imperative that our churches embrace and then inspire young, African American women to see themselves as they were created to be, the crown of creation. As I drive through block after block of inner-city streets, I see a wasteland of young, African American women in need of what God has equipped our churches with, a father's love and a mother's model of virtue. Sandra, in reality, did not create the environment that eventually led her to a life of drug addiction. It was created by the inactivity of the church. It was created by the lack of vision for young women on behalf of inner-city pastors, the lack of real passion to save young women on behalf of ministers' wives, the lack of inspiration on behalf of deaconesses to do anything above their ceremonial duties, and the failure of fathers to be fathers and mothers to be mothers. Finally, the environment that led to the destruction of the sweet little girl who arrived in Union Station on her mother's arm some 40 years ago was not so much the city, but rather the church in the city and its intoxication with itself. The church's desire to construct impressive, lavish, and elaborately decorated monuments to itself, instead of equipping an army of committed soldiers who will fight on behalf of the least, the lost, and left out is the real culprit behind the spiritual demise of this present generation. In retrospect, I see clearly that the problem was not Sandra, nor entirely the city. The problem was and is the church and its failure to meet the urban challenge.

CHAPTER ONE
A DEACONESS BIRTHED BY PAIN

Deaconess Jones

My deaconess ministry had its genesis in pain. I clearly remember how the pain began. It began at the early, innocent, and vulnerable age of 13 with the abandonment of my father. That abandonment was never adequately explained by my very private, proud, and pugnacious mother, "Big Frances." In the absence of an explanation, I, "Little Frances," was left to grapple with my abandonment from an adolescent prospective. Such a perspective caused me to succumb to the tendency to blame myself for my father's leaving. Subsequently, I spent the remainder of my formative teen years in a kind of semi, self-imposed isolation, or as I call it—my period of "solitary confinement." During this isolation period, I lucidly remember feelings of loneliness, although I was seldom alone. I lived in a household with my boisterously angry mother and brother, with whom I never felt close. This period was accented by periodic visits from my callously glib aunts who were never without emotionally devastating words that destroyed any sense of self-esteem that was left in the wake of the abandonment of my father, whom I adored. The constant and callous criticism that I experienced as a result of a Southern culture that seemed to thrive on humbling Negro children created a very toxic and dysfunctional environment for a young girl already grappling with her father's absence and abandonment. In addition to these sources of degradation, I was fair-skinned, which was, in my mind, ethnic stigma—even in what was considered the post-Jim Crow era. The full-bodied "birthmark" of fair skin almost always guaranteed any description of such a person as "high yellow." "High yellow niggers" were always thought to think themselves better than regular "niggers." The mere sight of "high yellow niggers" always seemed a reminder of the perceived social superiority implied by the daily viewing of "white only" signs that no nigger who could read could ever escape. To be "high yellow" in South Carolina in the 40s and 50s ensured that one would be the recipient of the Southern Negro anger for the ill treatment of the "colored." I was no exception. By virtue of my complexion, I was automatically the target of tart jokes and tawdry teasing.

My deaconess ministry had its genesis in pain.

In addition to the stigma of a high-yellow complexion, I was an even bigger target of verbally abusive sarcasm because of my height. My 5-feet 7-inch-thin frame, along with my budding embarrassing "bustiness" at the age of 15, caused this awkwardly growing teenager to become extremely self-conscious and conspicuously shy. My shyness only served to make me a natural and convenient target for people, especially adult family members who needed an outlet for their own frustration without fear of retaliation. Therefore, in such a time as the early 50s, and in such desperate places as the ghettos of urban Charlotte, North Carolina, Negroes on the bottom rung of the social ladder, to put it mildly, caught hell. This hell was not ill intentioned, for it was merely an effort to cope with the limitations of racial discrimination and economic degradation. It was anger turned on each other, just a means of emotional survival. Such was the social climate in which I was forced to grow up.

Living daily within this kind of environment was painful and emotionally traumatic, and it does something ugly and cruel to an impressionable young woman. In my effort to survive, emotionally and psychologically, I developed a knack for the quick verbal comeback, limited, of course, to my peers. I enjoyed no such privilege with the grown folks, for such defensive verbal retorts would have been interpreted as efforts to sass and a blatant sign of disrespect that would demand an instant backhand. It was, however, the grown folks who inflicted the pain that would shape not only my life but the lives of my children, as well. It was the grown folks who created an atmosphere that made me vulnerable for victimization by anyone who decided to take advantage of my vulnerability. Truly, it was the daily *adult* sarcastic stabs that would cause the internal bleeding that only began to subside with a relationship with Christ. My relationship with Christ, however, did not come in time to stem the legacy of pain that passed from my elders through me to my offspring. Consequently, it was my offspring who compounded my pain as an adult. I admit: it was the very fruit of my abused womb who forced me to confront the demons that could not be diminished or drowned by the tide of time that would flow through the length and breathe of my life. But thanks to God, from such a painful tide flowed a life that I have not only survived, but a life through which I have also given birth to a ministry that attacks the very demons that seek to nullify the truth of the gospel.

****

Wounded Woman on the Run

Pastor McCoy

We begin our journey nine days before Fran's sixtieth birthday, as she convalesced from a mild stroke. While it has been my lot to listen to her pain, it has been her lot to *live* her pain. There were moments of prayer and counsel, but mostly, it was my task to simply listen and encourage her on her journey. During the turbulence of her journey, I have often been but a bystander, watching in awe as God has moved in the midst of the storms of her life as she endured incredible pain and long nights when it seemed the journey would have no sane end. William Ernest Henley writes in his poem "Invictus," "In the fell clutch of circumstance, I have not winced nor cried aloud / Under the bludgeoning of chance, My head is bloody, but unbowed."[1] While experiencing Fran's journey alongside her as her pastor, I have witnessed the awesome movement of God in the ebbs and surges of the tides of her life, and she has been a remarkable testimony to the keeping power of Christ.

Deaconess Jones

Initially, I attempted to suppress the hurt that cheapened my existence with anger. "How could a father, my father, just leave and erase me from his mind and eradicate our relationship from his heart?" I asked myself. "How could my daddy just dump me as if I were useless waste or dead weight? Was I that repulsive, that disgusting, that much of a pest, that embarrassing to claim as a daughter?" At that time in my life, I was not at a good place emotionally. In an effort to get the affection that I lost in my father's abandonment, I became sexually promiscuous, which resulted in two unplanned pregnancies. Then, in order to run from the shame of being an unwed mother, I relocated from Charlotte, North Carolina to Washington, DC. In Washington, DC, I attempted to medicate my hurt and shame, first with alcohol—the party life—and then with church. Finally, after 40 years of dealing with the pain and madness of what theologians label as "secular humanism," seeking morality and peace through human intelligence, I embraced Christ. But then I learned how utterly difficult it is to totally "let go and let God," especially when the residual effects of one's past continue to dog and dominate one's life. Through it all, however, I possessed an undying conviction that the secret to human wholeness and spiritual prosperity was rightly dividing the Word of God in a world gone mad. I did not know, however, that the road to completely trusting the Christ I embrace would run through the hospital doors of Prince George's Community Hospital.

The day was August 11, 2002, and I was dying in a hospital bed in Cheverly, Maryland. However, I was not sad because I was dying. I was not depressed because I was dying. My 60th birthday was 9 days away, and I was making a conscious decision to die. I was deciding to die because I had come to the realization that I would not live to celebrate the next decade of my life, unless I died. Therefore, in choosing to die, I was choosing to live.

It was a Sunday, and ordinarily, I would have been sitting in church worshipping and praising God. I realize now, however, that I would have been praising a God whom I had never fully allowed to be God. Within the two days of my admittance to the hospital suffering from chest pains, I believe God showed me exactly how I arrived to that second floor, semi-private room. I arrived there, not by ambulance, although such was the mode of transportation, but I had arrived there by a lack of trust in the One I called my Lord and Savior. As the hospital staff shuffled me from one X-ray room to another, the most critical examination was taking place on a much higher realm. While I lie awaiting the flash of yet another X-ray, my entire life of distrust in God flashed quietly before me. With each flicker rushed forth another restless revelation of an area that I had not entrusted unto the One who beckoned me a quarter of a century before to "Come unto Me and I will give you rest" (Matthew 11:28). I realized that since I had met Jesus, some 25 years prior to that day, I had failed to "cast all of my cares upon Him" (I Peter 5:7). Consequently, how could I have been angry with God if I had never truly trusted God? My anger would have been misplaced, at best, for in my case, no one possessed the power to put me in a hospital bed but Frances Jones.

> My dairy entry: August 11, 2002
> *As I lie here, I believe that it is vitally important that I share my experience because I have witnessed countless women in this same dilemma, dying the same slow, torturous death. I see now that it is suicide to attempt to compete with Jesus as Savior. Jesus is the only One who can say, "Come unto me and I will give you rest." "My yoke is easy and my burden is light." I am convinced that across this country, sadly in the kingdom of Christianity, there are many women who are destroying themselves under the same suicidal yoke as I, for they are physically, emotionally, and psychologically collapsing under the same burdens as I for the past 40 years. They are seeking to endure the hardships as heads of families and principle caretakers of their elderly parents and errant children under they own strength. Therefore, the fastest growing single group of people suffering from heart disease in America is women. And even as I lie here, I see women being taken on hospital*

gurneys in and out of ICU and to get EKGs and MRIs, visibly breaking down under the stress of the savior-complex that plagues too many of us who claim that title reserved for Jesus alone. Many of us women have even been blessed with responsible husbands yet refuse to let go of the stress in our lives, thinking that only we can save our children or bring deliverance to those persons whom we are literally loving to death. Our blessed Savior, in His providential care, has given us men—who only need our permission to be men—but we continue to castrate them. Many of us have men who are eager to shoulder much of the stress that we unilaterally shoulder, but we obstinately refuse and selfishly continue to resist such help. We have contracted the savior-complex, and it is sucking the very life out of our souls. I encourage all women who struggle under the mistaken notion that they can save those they love to take it from a woman lying in a lonely hospital room that the sandals of the Savior are too big for 10,000 women, let alone just one. I am rapidly coming to the conclusion that for my own sake and sanity, and for persons to whom I serve as "savior," I must abdicate the throne of Christ and strip myself of the misplaced title of Messiah.

It is vitally important that I chronicle my ascendency to the lofty realm of deity. Plain and simple, I have had a drug problem for over 25 years. Yes, you heard it right! Fran Jones, celebrated author and honored president of the deaconess ministry at her church, has quietly struggled with substance abuse for more than a quarter of a century. My struggle has drained my household financial resources, and it has taken an immeasurable toll on my marriage. It has stolen the most valuable years of my life. My struggle with drugs has taken me into some of the most dangerous neighborhoods in the inner city, into crack houses and dimly lit alleys. My drug problem has forced me to conduct business with some of the most frightening characters in the drug community—petty dealers seeking to make names for themselves by enforcing their unwritten rules by the most violent means necessary. Menacing figures, shrouded and lurking in the shadows, who went by the names of "BO," "Big Dog," "Little Man," "Booger," and "Butch the Butcher." My drug problem has caused me to hypocritically sit in church worship service and sing, "On Christ the solid rock I stand," while inwardly bowing before the altar of the crack rock. My drug problem has allowed me to conduct deaconess seminars while at the same time conduct financial transactions in the demonic world of "smack," "crack," and "angel dust." Sadly, I have taken money that was given me to bless God and given it to a culture that undercuts the very activity of God in the world today. Now, before you leap to the obvious conclusion, my drug problem was not a result of any direct addiction on my behalf, for I have not so much as engaged in social drinking over the past 25 years. My "drug problem" was actually a loved one's addiction. Though I have never purchased illegal drugs, I have, in some shape, form, or fashion, paid off many drug debts for which I am ashamed. I was the perfect parent and, therefore, the perfect enabler. My actions were a result of, in many ways, misplaced guilt on my behalf. From such guilt I must, for the sake of my life, declare and claim my freedom.

How different, I thought, from the life I had imagined for myself approaching my 60th birthday. As a woman who had worked all her life, I looked forward to a retirement full of leisure, travel, enjoying and spoiling my grandchildren, and just enjoying the fruit of my labor. I was especially looking forward to exercising my spiritual gift and teaching other young women how to walk in Christ. As an author of several books and articles on the role of the Baptist deaconess, I carried within my bosom a passion for sharing with others the blessings that God had so bountifully granted me. But there I was, lying in a hospital bed, being informed that I had suffered a "minor stroke," as if any such life-altering diagnosis could be classified as "minor." This *minor* stroke was having a *major* impact on my mental state. To put it bluntly, utilizing a phrase that I seldom use, I was "pissed off." I was pissed off because I had allowed someone else to cause me to have a stroke. I had allowed my child to do to me what I had refused to allow any man to do. In my past, I have fought, scratched, jumped out of windows, and even threatened bodily harm to any man who so much as hinted that he harbored any thought of touching one hair on my nappy head! Yet, at nearly 60 years old, I had allowed myself to be imprisoned by bars symbolized as IV tubes, hospital intercoms, tasteless hospital food, screams of "NURSE, NURSE," and a putrid smell that no disinfectant in the world can eliminate. I was pissed off, and just as appalling as the term itself, the anger that welled within my sanctified soul was ten times as unpleasant. The drug problem of my daughter had indeed metastasized from a cancer called "Control!" Control is how a mother seeks to address the issues of a grown child, as if the child were still 12. Control goes further than knowing what is best, for what is best is obvious. Control is the desire to determine how best to achieve that which is best. Control is snatching the reins of what *seems* to be a runaway life out of God's hands and seeking to single-handedly stop what only God can stop. Such actions always leave the people seeking control exasperated, frustrated, and somewhat out of control themselves.

Frances Jones had not been a good steward over Frances Jones. My reasons for doing so went much deeper than a cardiac probe or X-ray could ever reach. They were spiritual in nature. The only instrument that could probe deeply enough to cut away the tumor that was threatening my life was the Word of God, which was sharper than any *two-edged scalpel.*

This book is designed to engage in exploratory cardiac surgery to determine why I, 25 years into my walk with Christ, decided to compete with Him as Savior. I set forth to write this book because I know that I am not alone. I am representative of millions of women and men who profess a belief and trust in God but who unconsciously usurp His authority as the great physician, Jehovah Rophe. As we embark upon our journey, a journey that will prayerfully cause us to abdicate the throne of God, I must admit that the journey to my abdication only began on the examination table in Prince George's Hospital, but it continued at my kitchen table, nine days later, in the twilight of my 60th birthday, August 20, 2002.

There I languished, disappointed, sitting alone at my kitchen table in the closing hour of my 60th birthday. There I sat, in the painful, vice-like grips of guilt. Ideally, I should have been feeling the exuberance of being immensely blessed and highly favored, for not many people live to see their 60th birthday with a reasonable portion of good health. I should have been in the posture of prayer, thanking the Lord for the blessing of six decades of life. Honesty, however, requires from all of us truth, and the truth of the matter is, even with the numerous telephone calls, gifts, flowers, and birthday cards, I was miserable. I have always associated the words "happy" and "birthday" as identical twins, but on my 60th birthday, they seemed to be total strangers.

That day had dawned with such promise. The warm, August morning sun seemed to kiss me with seductive anticipation. After all, I was 60 and feeling great. I was 60 and possessed the

American Dream. I was 60 and was married to a loving, hard-working husband. I was 60 and was in the Lord, and He was in me. What more could I possibly ask for? As the sun set on my 60th year on planet earth, and the nocturnal whispers of yet another day could be heard in the inner chambers of my saved, but severely empty soul, I sat in solitude at the kitchen table of a house that any women would be proud of and searched for answers that perhaps no mere human could answer without divine intervention: Why had the "peace that surpasses all understanding" evaded my grasp? Why had the satisfaction of longevity not saturated the inner reaches of my being? The answer that echoes, in retrospect, makes itself so clear and reveals itself only as it steps out of the dark shadows of protective denial, "Addiction!" Addiction was the inescapable culprit that cast a hideously frightening gloom over what should have been a day full of the unrestrained laughter of celebration. Twenty years of drug addiction had doomed me to yet another year of frustration and agonizing anguish. Once again, drug addiction had kicked me in the teeth on what should have been a blissful birthday. Twenty years of drug addiction had depleted the limited resources that could have made possible the birthday bash that I had subconsciously planned for several years. Drug addiction had left me nearly financially and spiritually bankrupt. Drug addiction had taken a hold of my life and would not let go. It strangled the life out of what I considered the limited time I had left. The milestone of 60 does not guarantee the milestone of retirement at 65 or the promised reward of 3 score and 10. In reality, 60 is more than a milestone to be celebrated; it is a sober reminder of how time is a frightening thief that threatens to rob us women of that which makes us women, especially in the sight of a world that has a love affair with smooth skin and a youthful figure. For every time our husbands take a double take at some young honey in a mini-skirt, or momentarily linger as they thumb through the latest edition of the *Sports Illustrated Swimsuit Issue*, those of us women who are in the neighborhood of 60 die a little inside.

Such were the thoughts that raced in and out of my head as I sat at my dining room table reflecting on my life at 60 years of age. Time surely becomes an enemy and a friend, and certainly a priceless commodity, at 60. It becomes an enemy that threatens us with the herald of physical decline in the not-so-distant future. It becomes a friend in that it is a valued tutor of wisdom that cannot seem to come from any other source. It becomes a priceless commodity because every day, every hour, is more valuable than stock in IBM. As I sat in my well-furnished home, I began to channel my anger toward the source of my drug problem, which was the person who had caused my life to be in limbo for the past 20 years, my eldest daughter. It was she who had brought such unseemly characters as Bo, Jay, Big Dog, and Little Man to the doorstep of my life. Even now, nine years removed from my 60th birthday and the horrors of that situation, I shudder when I think of the darkness that such shady characters brought into my life. The money I wasted, directly or indirectly, supporting my daughter's drug addiction or paying off some of her drug debts because of some real or perceived threat to her life, could have made my retirement a little less economically challenged. So, in retrospect, I see clearly that during the twilight of my 60th birthday, the culprit that I was really wrestling with at my dining room table was Anger. I was angry with myself, with my daughter, and with her husband.

The anger I was experiencing with myself was simply that I had allowed myself to be caught in such a predicament. In actuality, that predicament was more like a cage that had me on the outside of life looking in. The time I had left on the planet was being limited by someone other than God or Frances. I now realize that to allow anyone else to cage us is idolatry, plain and simple. God has given each of us the ability to control our own destiny under His limitless power. God and God alone should possess the power to limit us. No human being should be given such God-like power.

Secondly, I was angry with my daughter, for I was under the erroneous and misguided opinion that she could control her actions. It is only in retrospect that I have realized that her life was under the demonic control of a cruel lord who had her chained to the heavy millstone of drug addiction. I have discovered that Satan is indeed subtle. He possesses the ability to keep his victims spiritually and emotionally weighed down by wrapping so many emotional issues around a millstone that we sink in an attempt to free ourselves. As I sought to free my daughter from drowning under the weight of her millstone, guilt threatened to take me under. Therefore, my attempts to gain my daughter's freedom entangled me with the tentacles of my own emotional and spiritual issues. Such issues made me what drug counselors call an "enabler" or "co-dependent." I now have come to believe that such is true, in most cases, wherein a parent grapples with a child's addiction. It is difficult for a parent not to slowly drift to the hellish conclusion that somehow, somewhere along the line, the state of the child is a direct result of something she or he has done or did not do in the raising of that child. Perhaps I shouldn't have taken that part-time job that took time away from my child. Perhaps I should have never re-married; perhaps I should have taken her to see more Disney, hired Mary Poppins, or enrolled her into a charter school. Maybe if I had spent more time helping with homework, or a thousand other parent-child activities, things would have turned out differently. As a parent of a child addicted to drugs, one finds oneself in a constant state of second-guessing and "what-ifing," so much so until instead of being aggressive in seeking treatment, one perpetuates the problem. All the while, the child sinks deeper and deeper into the dark abyss of addiction as the parent sinks deeper and deeper into depression and self-recrimination. Worst yet, if that parent is in regular attendance at church, or perhaps even a high profile church officer, the prideful testimonies of parents who have children in college and doing well work as stinging darts and damnable indictments. The parent of the addicted child finds it difficult, if not impossible, to escape the agonizing feelings of failure and direct responsibility for the dysfunctional state of the child. Such feelings cause the parent of the addicted child to vacillate between loving and loathing the thought of one's own child. What is it that is so powerful that it can cause a mother to sometimes loathe the thought of the child of her womb? The demonic effects of long-term drug addiction. In the twilight of my 60th birthday, I had reached that wretched no man's land where I couldn't give a rats behind if my daughter lived or died. Death seemed the only way to freedom on the night I turned 60.

To add fuel to the raging, out-of-control fire of anger, as if things could not have gotten any worse, my son-in-law had allowed the beast of drug addiction to invade his life. Thus, I was dealing with drug addiction times two. My toddler grandchildren were not only cursed with a mother addicted to drugs, but a father, as well. In retrospect, as I reflect on that night just over eight years ago, I realize that it could have been no one but the Lord who brought such a tragic farce to a conclusion. As I read the account of my thoughts on that evening in my diary, it all seemed so surreal. My diary on my 60th birthday read as follows:

The thing that ticks me off is that my daughter has allowed herself to just stop living. She is in no condition to go back to school to get an education so she can take care of herself, or her own children. It angers me for people to pity her and me. She feels that she has to take verbal abuse because she has no hope. If she would spend as much time on positive things for herself and her children instead of dragging her sorry behind from one crack house to another getting high, she would be a source to be reckoned with. But no, she has to wallow in despair...

For the past few days the calls have been coming, "Ma, how are you feeling? When you did not answer the phone, I thought something was wrong." Well, whoopdedo!!! How many days and nights have I called, got no answer, and yes, something was wrong? Now you call to tell me where you are going and when you are getting back. Why not before? I ask myself. Why not before you carelessly sapped the life out of me? Why? Why? I have so many questions that I guess will never be answered on this side, but still I move on in the light of Jesus Christ. He is my source and strength, a refuge for all I have to endure.

Before I complete my reflections on the night of my 60th birthday, I must address the periods in which the "ebb tide." They were times of great, deceptive hope. During the 20 years that my daughter suffered from addictions, there were lulls that promised an end to the ordeal. There were months, even years, of sobriety that hope sprang anew. There were times when my sweet Sandra would return and bring a joy that caused my spirit to soar. These are the periods that live on in my heart as I think of my now deceased child. There has never been, nor will there ever be, anyone in my life like Sandra. She was so loving, so optimistic, so full of life when she was . . . Sandra. No one could bring me as much joy as she. No one enjoyed life like Sandra. She was such a loving daughter, a loving mother, and a loving wife. When Sandra loved, she loved.

Sandra was also a very naïve person. Sandra trusted anyone. She was hospitable to everyone. I sincerely believe that her naïveté was a major contributing factor to her drug addiction. She was so naïve until I think she honestly believed the person who first uttered the words, "Take a hit of this. It won't harm you." I have often wondered if that person, whoever he or she is, ever thinks of the damage such an invitation has caused in the lives of so many. I have often wondered if that person, whoever he or she is, has any idea how much hurt, how much anguish, and how beautiful of a life was destroyed just by uttering such words. There is one thing, however, that I do know. Whoever first uttered those words to my teenaged daughter snuffed out a life that was beautiful, priceless, and precious and is just as responsible for her death as the person who murdered her some 20 years later.

The lulls in her drug usage would give me great hope that the addiction was a thing of the past, especially because they were reinforced by her very passionate religious faith. I know that it seems paradoxical for me to contend that Sandra possessed a passionate religious faith, but she did. She was naïvely religious. Her religious faith was so strong that even though it was publically known that she had relapsed back into drug addiction, she would return to the church time and time again. Even at times when I, as her mother and president of the deaconesses, was completely embarrassed by her presence in the church and inwardly prayed she would not respond to the invitation for rededication or the altar call, my embarrassment and prayers were in vain. Whenever the altar call was extended, she would get up amidst all of the glaring, cynical, and sarcastic murmurings of the self-righteous saints of God, and I must admit that I would become angry with the way she believed many of those "saints" that I knew were hypocritically encouraging her. Her naïveté, however, caused her to accept their encouragement as if it were genuine. Her very strong religious faith would compel her time and time again to believe time and time again that God would heal her addiction. Such a roller coaster ride of relapse and repentance slowly, but surely, began to take its toll on my spiritual strength.

I have always, since I embraced Jesus, considered myself to be a strong woman, able to take life's most painful blows and keep on kicking. Then, after knowing the Lord Jesus Christ as Redeemer, I felt that I was a powerhouse. In Him, I could do all things, but this one thing had a grip on me that sometimes hindered even *my* praises to God. I used to wonder, "How in the world did this strong black woman from North Carolina raise and care for two children on her own and then succumb to the weight of drug addiction? How in God's name could a strong woman like Frances, who was so strong that she was able to relocate to another city with just two girls and $24 dollars, allow something as cheap as crack cocaine to stuff out her praise? I had made it without my father, who abandoned me, without my babies' daddy, who walked away, yet I was allowing some jerk like Bo Bo the drug dealer to break me down like an unbeliever and reduce me to an emotional wreck. Addiction, and all that goes with it, was more than I could handle. It took me up and dropped me into a free fall in ways I had never dreamed. It created a hell from which there seemed no escape.

CHAPTER TWO
MEETING THE URBAN CHALLENGE—
THE NEED FOR STREET-WISE DEACONESSES

"Behold, I sent you forth as sheep in the midst of wolves: be ye therefore wise as serpents" (Matthew 10:16a)

Deaconess Jones

The atmosphere around bus stations in most inner cities is always somewhat dark, dismal, desperate, and unseemly. Unlike the atmosphere surrounding airports, and to a lesser degree train depots, which are more professional and pristine, the bus depot is often the entry point of the most vulnerable female traveler. One does not have to study long to decipher that females who travel alone from the South by bus, rather than air, are somewhat financially strapped and limited in their knowledge of big cities. Their mere appearance shouts "country bumpkin." Out of the shadows of such a setting, along with the faint, putrid odor of urine, lurks the "Bus Depot Predator"—waiting to pounce upon the unsuspecting, naïve young woman from "Small Town, USA" looking for a new start in the city. Perhaps she has arrived to attend the city college or simply to start life afresh. She attempts to attire herself in a way that defies her rural origin, but to the keen-eyed predator, her perceived city clothing is but a costume, a futile attempt to blend in and masquerade as a native city dweller. She may as well have "vulnerable" tattooed on her forehead. She has no idea that she is about to be taken on the most dangerous ride of her life.

The predator's approach is always casual. She readily mistakes him as a friendly, helpful good guy giving directions. He is a welcome relief, God's promised angel in a strange and scary place. He seems so willing to help, so helpful with her tattered bags. He offers assistance to the cabstand. He is as considerate as a railroad redcap. She thinks to herself, "God always provides a ram in the bush." He gives her every impression that he is headed for the cabstand, but his real destination is his own automobile parked nearby. Very casually, he inquires as to what part of town she is trying to get to. And isn't it just like the Lord to provide a person who lives in just that part of town? It doesn't take long for her to calculate and appreciate the cab fare she would be saving. It takes an even shorter time for him to offer her the most expensive ride of her life. The rest is the history of too many young women from Small town, USA. It is a sad commentary of young women still wet behind the ears. Such young women are but an unwise decision away from lives washed down the toilets of big cities. The sheer nature of life in the inner city often forces uneducated African American men into a life of survival via exploiting their own. Poverty breeds desperation, and desperation seizes the moment and the easiest prey. So often, what begins in her mind as the possibility of a fresh start and the beginning of a beautiful love affair ends as multi-sex propositions, pimping arrangements, prostitution, drug addiction, or at the very least, another broken heart and shattered dream.

Now, let's rewind the videotape. What if when that late night Greyhound bus rolled into the bus depot and little Miss Naïve Country Bumpkin alighted she were met by a street-wise deaconess, instead of "Mr. Helpful" or some other stranger with motives that are suspect? What if that deaconess provided that young woman a ride to her destination, kept in contact with her during that week, and picked her up for church that next Sunday? What if . . . ? What if . . . ? So many lives ride on the what-if train. How different would the lives of young women be *if* they were embraced by deaconesses instead of devious and devilish street predators looking for a means to get paid? We must learn from the past. Many churches in inner cities are filled with women who arrived once under the aforementioned circumstances. They knew no one, and therefore, fell prey to predators. The horror stories are endless. I often wonder how differently my life, and the lives of my daughters, especially my slain daughter, would have been *if I were met by a dedicated, street-wise, hospitable deaconess*. What if I had been shown the ropes by a street-wise deaconess instead of the incorrigible men who don't even merit mention? I had no idea that among the beautiful and stately national monuments, museums, and landmarks of our nation's capital lurked predators of the most grievous kind. I hadn't the faintest notion that in what some call the greatest city in the world, there were

> *How different would the lives of young women be if they were embraced by deaconesses instead of devious and devilish street predators looking for a means to get paid?*

such good-looking men with such bad intentions, men who would physically abuse me, men who would entice my child to experiment with illicit drugs and one day leave her dying on a bathroom floor, bleeding profusely from a stab wound to the neck. Sadly, the perpetrator of this crime is still at large, still out there, somewhere, perhaps awaiting yet another female victim. Perhaps she will be your daughter, your niece, or the "smart as a whip" scholarship recipient in your church. I cannot speak for other deaconesses in other churches, but I can emphatically say, "Never again!" *Not on my watch, at my church. Not if I can help it. No more will I sit idly by and look the other way as some naïve young woman is victimized by a known church predator.* We all know who the church predators are, and we all are well aware of how they stalk their prey. To do nothing is to be complicit in their sin. I believe it is time to sound the alarm, rally the troops, and put an end to such boldness right under the shadow of the cross of Christ.

Today's deaconesses must be street-wise. Our Lord admonishes those He sends forth to minister to those most vulnerable, and He sends us forth in the midst of wolves. Therefore, we must be "wise as serpents" (Matt. 10:16).

What if . . . ?

What if a network could be established between churches from the South and churches in big cities to ensure the safety and welfare of young people, in general, and young women, in particular? What if churches in Small Town, USA networked with churches in large college towns? Such networking would ensure that young church freshmen who arrive each fall to attend school would not be overwhelmed by the bright lights of the big city but would have a support system, a church family, and help with securing employment. Most African American church members of Northern and Western congregations have ties to churches "back home." It would not be difficult to establish a contact to remind pastors back home of the dangers of sending their young people to schools in larger cities without having a support system. Just as schools are preparing students to excel academically, churches ought to be preparing students to survive spiritually and socially. On scholarship award days, deaconesses ought to immediately get busy networking with churches of like faith and doctrine in the city the awardee intends to attend school. The question, "Have you found a church yet?" ought never to be asked by a parent or church leader back home. Deaconesses must become creative in their approach to urban ministry. Jesus encourages us to be "wise as serpents" (Matt. 10:16). Just as a serpent waits patiently for its prey, Jesus waited for the woman to come to the well in John's gospel. Unlike a serpent, however, who would have seized the opportunity to inject the woman with deadly venom, Jesus empowered her with living water (John 4:14). Likewise, we must learn the techniques and approaches of the Adversary and beat him to the punch. No longer should we wait for emotionally injured young people to somehow randomly stumble through the doors of our churches bleeding from the wounds inflicted on the mean streets of our cities. We must become proactive and obey the commission of Jesus to "go" (Matthew 28:19). The biblical attitude of hospitality to the stranger must be applied in a more effective way if we are going to protect the daughters of our people who leave small towns seeking a better life in big cities. We cannot continue to allow young women to become a part of the negative statistics that so many others have succumbed to.

I recommend that your next deaconess meeting be held at your local bus depot. Get a schedule. When buses arrive from the cities of the South, observe the arrival of starry-eyed, innocent young women, perhaps with small children, fully aware of the life they left in Small Town, USA but totally unaware of the dangers that lie ahead in the big city. Fast forward now, and envision one of these women sitting on the back row of your church, quietly weeping. Are such tears preventable? Only God knows.

A deaconess must be street-wise because shady and seductive street predators do not limit their devilish activity to the streets. I distinctly remember my pastor, when teaching a Church History class, say that "when the devil discovered that he could not defeat the church, he joined the church." Ideally, the church should be a place of safety. However, all who are a part of a church are not void of the street mentality. Some of the greatest wounds that can be inflicted upon young, naïve women can occur right within the sanctified walls of the church. In today's inner-city church, wolves have been known to masquerade in sheep's clothing. Does not Jesus warn us in Matthew 7:15 to "Beware of false prophets, which come to you in sheep's clothing, but inwardly they are ravening wolves?" Because they are in the church, they are in the perfect position to get closer to their prey and sink their teeth in deeper. Some may think, "After all, that's Deacon Brown's son. He's okay." However, the deaconess must be ever vigilant, for not all the brothers who sing in the choir or sit on the deacon's bench or serve on the Trustee Board can be trusted. Nor do all the young men in the church have the spiritual maturity to say "no" to the flesh or the insight to fully comprehend the emotional damage they can cause by manipulating the feelings of young women for their ego's sake. I am fully aware that not all such manipulation is intentional, but all manipulation is hurtful to the manipulated. I have personally witnessed men in positions of trust in the church devour young women right under the watchful eyes of the shepherd. Some of the most sadistic and perverted behavior has been displayed by church predators. Sadly, they are often allowed to operate unimpeded in the house of God. Often, the conduct of young men is not held to any minimum standard and unacceptable behavior is tolerated just to keep young men in the church. And if a young man has some musical ability, he is often given carte blanche to have his way in the house of God. Yes, we must encourage young men to stay in the church, but the church must not tolerate the victimization of the naïve just to keep men coming. The street-wise deaconess must not look the other way when she witnesses some young, naïve woman being seduced by a church predator. A good deaconess is not discouraged from acting on the behalf of a young woman simply because she is told, "Mind your own business," even by the young woman. Young women *are* the business of deaconesses.

I am not suggesting that a deaconess be a busybody, butting into all the relationships of young people in the church. I am suggesting that deaconesses cultivate such relationships of trust that when the deaconess cries wolf, the sheep will at least take notice. It is important that deaconess cry wolf before young women fall in love because by then, it is too late. By then, all a deaconess can do is remain in a position of influence because sooner or later, the prey will need prayer and a strong, loving shoulder upon which to lean.

CHAPTER THREE
MEETING THE URBAN CHALLENGE—
NOT FOR DEACONESSES ONLY

He [the Lord] shall turn the heart of the fathers to the children" (Malachi 4:6b)

Deaconess Jones

As I look back over the life of my daughter, I have come to understand that the issues that contributed to her life of addiction were many. As I continue to loose myself from the shackles of guilt that tend to haunt most parents of young people who have fallen into a life of drug addiction, and all that comes with it, I have begun to see more clearly that the beast that devoured my child possessed many heads. First and foremost, I believe the roots that bore the bitter fruit of her pain began with the men associated with her life. I am well aware that this may sound as if I am playing the male card as I engage in the blame game, but as I peruse the pages of her life, I see a pattern. This pattern weaves a disturbingly ugly web of disappointment that began with the abandonment of *my* father, *her* father, and all the men in our lives up until I married my husband. In my study and observation of women, I have come to recognize that the chief motivation and primary focus in the lives of women is men. Almost from birth, females are driven by the need for the protection of males, the validation of males, the acclamation of males, and the affection of males. As little girls, we need the strength of fathers to feel physically secure. From adolescence through adulthood, we need the validation of men to feel emotionally secure. As young women, we need the acclamation of men to feel attractive. As women moving through the seasons of our lives, in order to feel like women whose lives matter, we need affection. With these truths, the real salvation of women begins with men.

Therefore, as deaconesses, our first step in ministry to women is to teach fathers their importance in the lives of their daughters. As the curtains of the Old Testament closed some 2,000 years ago, a 400 year hush came over the people of God. I believe that such a period of relative silence on the part of heaven was for the distinct purpose of allowing men to ponder their role in the lives of their children, for if mankind were to emerge from the nocturnal agony of the dysfunctional spiritual condition, a new generation of fathers had to be awakened to their responsibilities insofar as their children were concerned. If humanity was ever going to commune with divinity, the most basic unit, the family, was going to have to be the focus of fathers. As the curtains have lifted upon a new age in which God is represented as Father, the role of earthly fathers must also be redefined. It is incumbent upon deaconesses to encourage fathers in the church to mirror the love of "our Father which art in heaven" (Matt. 6:9). In some churches, this will prove to be a problem because some men resist the effort, on the behalf of women, to teach men. For this reason, it is important for deaconesses to cultivate a close bond with their pastors. If the church is going to be effective in the area of women's ministry, women's ministry must be a major part of the vision of our pastors. It is next to impossible for deaconesses to impact women to any great degree if a ministry to reach and empower women is not a priority of the pastor. Pastors must not just give lip service to the empowerment of women. Pastors, especially male pastors, must demonstrate a consistent passion for the welfare of women, especially young women. This can be done without the degradation of men. Men must be strongly encouraged to embrace their daughters, regardless of their relationship with their daughters' mothers. Ideally, two parents in the home should be the norm, but we are living in the 21st century. Therefore, we must be realistic. At least 63% of African American children live in a single-parent home, and the overwhelming majority of the cases show that the single parent with whom they reside is the mother, according to Sharon Leverett, of the Single Black Parents website. This fact should not excuse fathers from being actively involved in the lives of their daughters. Daughters are aching for their fathers. Daughters are compromising their morals to get the cheap substitute for fatherly affection. Daughters are growing up seeking an inordinate amount of male attention because their fathers act as if they do not exist. My life is a prime example of the lack of a father in a young girl's life. It seems that when my father divorced my mother, he divorced me. He was the lord of my life, the center of my universe, the anchor that represented stability in my life. Perhaps if I had just one deaconess in my life, she could have helped me to find an anchor that held and gripped the solid rock of Christ. If such had been the case, my life may not have begun to spiral out of control the moment he divorced our family. My sense of selfhood vanished in the days following his unannounced departure. I was devastated beyond repair. That devastation created chaos in my life. That devastation produced two daughters out of wedlock. That devastation greatly affected the way I saw my children and myself. Through the life of my daughters, the devastation continued. The negative effects of the lack of a grandfather, combined with the absence of a father, were clearly evident in the way my daughters saw themselves. Optimistic psychologists can say what they will, but I contend that it is impossible for a mother to adequately raise strong and self-sufficient sons and daughters in the absence of their father. The strength that a father provides cannot be substituted by the strongest of mothers. The sense of security that a father gives cannot be duplicated by any other source. Just as I looked for my father until the day that I heard he had died, I sincerely believe that Sandra searched for her father all the days of her life. I believe that she rejected my husband as a stepfather because she was angry that he was attempting to replace her biological father. The closest figure she could find, insofar as a father was concerned, was her pastor. As I observed her interaction with him, or her response when she relapsed and heard his voice, I was amazed. Until the day of her death, she felt a great sense of validation because there was a man who, by choice, served as her father. If the church is going to be a salvation station for young women, pastors must lead the way in "turning the hearts of the fathers to their children" (Malachi 3:6a).

Our second step in ministry to women, in light of the resistance of men in the church to accept the teaching of women, is for deaconesses to impress upon pastors to lead men into a new respect of women. We must insist that pastors drum it into the heads of the men under their influence that women are more than the sum total of their body parts. It seems that since my father's abandonment, every man who has looked in my direction has seen my posterior before my person, my bulging breasts before my beautiful heart, and my slender legs before my spiritual walk. With this kind of mindset, as a woman's body diminishes, her worth diminishes. Since adulthood, I have encountered few men, even in the church, who see women as their equal. They may fain it, but deep down, men see women as inferior and not their peers. Up until the past decade, the church has been the primary perpetuator of this view of women. Just as the white preacher validated the white slave owner, the black preacher validates the degradation of women. If one listens closely and long enough, in some churches today, one can hear it when pastors preach—the subtle, subliminal message that women are not the equal of men. It will not be until the majority of male pastors mature to the point that *they* see women as equal to men that the message will become clear to other men. Until then, in men's eyes, women exist for the pleasure of men. Until then, the rightful place of the woman will be seen as under the man instead of beside the man. Until then, the deaconess will not enjoy the same status as the male deacon. Until then, women will continue to be marginalized in the very churches that they gave their blood, sweat, toil, and tears to build while men were "sowing their wild oats." When the message of inferiority comes from the place that is perceived as the podium of God, there can be but one interpretation—such is the position of God. Until then, Tyler Perry's character Madea will be a better friend of women than the pastors of our churches. We must remember that the year is 2011 A.D., not 2011 B.C.

Thirdly, if the church, which has been the womb that has birthed the inequities of men and women, is ever to correct its sin, it must create a climate that invites dialogue between men and women. The wise Solomon encourages us, "with all thy getting, get understanding" (Proverbs 4:7). I sincerely believe that the crux of the problems that keep the sexes worlds apart is that neither has any real knowledge of the other. I have been involved with the church all my life. I am a product of the church. I know the power of the church to impact lives. I have witnessed the church lead change instead of just responding to change. The church pulpit carries more power in the African American community than one can ever find on the floor of the Congress. It is unthinkable for the church to be silent at such time and with such a topic as this. Simply put, the church is sitting down on its power and allowing the powers that be to dictate and shape society. Therefore, I can make the statement that Martin L. King, Jr., made in 1967 as he led a protest march in Chicago against the war in Viet Nam, "I speak out against this war because I am disappointed in America. There can be no great disappointment where there is no great love."[1] My sentiments are the same. I speak out against the church's handling of the male/female issue because I am disappointed in the church. "There can be no great disappointment where there is no great love," and I, Fran Jones, love the church. I will always be a part of the church. The church has become my life, and because of my great love and attachment for the church, I desire for it to be all that God designed it to be—which is a true sanctuary for all of his children, *women included.* I honestly see the church as the last bastion of hope for understanding between the sexes. Such television shows as *Dr. Phil* and *Oprah* tend to sensationalize the issues instead of seeking solutions for the issues. Yes, infidelity exists. Mental and physical abuse is real, and men and women are tragically separated in their knowledge of each other. And, as sad and sadistic as it is, clergy and laity do get involved in sexual impropriety. And yes, there are men and women whose sexual appetites are so large until they eat themselves to death and in the process create a sexual gulf between themselves and their partners. Yes, Dr. Phil, women don't have to take it. Oprah, you are correct; she can just walk away. But I contend that until we get to the whys of these situations and set forth some spiritual basis for change, such will continue, and children will continue to be the tragic victims of dysfunctional families and victims of the power struggle between angry parents. As a woman who is sick and tired of tuning into talk TV for a daily dose of the issues that are tearing our families apart, I encourage the church to get involved. Cultivate some real dialogue beyond the range of the TV cameras where viewers seem to be in total awe as they wait to see if someone is going to get slapped. The days of Jerry Springer and Geraldo are over. Shows like *Sex in the City* and *Desperate Housewives* do nothing to solve the basic issues that men and women have—living in total ignorance of each other. If the church of today fails to bring men and women together and teach the truths that are only found in Scripture, it will continue to lose its relevance in a complex and ever-evolving society. The complex dynamics of the male-female relationship must become a regular part of the church's agenda. If the very first issue that God dealt with in the Holy Writ was the sexuality of human beings, why is sex so absent from the church's weekly menu? The church cannot effectively address spirituality if it does not sufficiently address sexuality. Such dialogues are occurring everywhere except where it should take place, and that is in the church. How can a topic like sex be so totally off the church's radar? What is the church trying to hide? Why is it so afraid to speak on the matters that mean the most to African American families?

I believe that the great problem in establishing dialogue between the sexes is that the church is confused between the roles of wives and the rights of women. Over the centuries, the male-dominated church has never clearly defined the specific role of women in marriage. What does "being under subjection" truly mean? Keeping your mouth shut and allowing a man to run the ship aground? Always being available for sex while the husband is seldom available for conversation? Allowing oneself to be an outlet for his anger but seldom an object of his affection? Forcing oneself to "dumb down" and keep silent when you know he is dead wrong and about to make a decision that concerns the welfare of you both? If the wife were your daughter, would you encourage her to assume such a subservient or sub-human role? What are the dynamics of a male/female relationship in this modern era? Who sets the rules when the wife is more spiritual than the husband? Who washes the dishes when the husband is unemployed and the wife is the principle breadwinner? At the very least, the church must provide some practical guidance on the roles of wives and the rights of women.

The Bible clearly states, "Wives ought to be obedient to their own husbands" (Titus 2:5), but does this mean that women who are not married ought to be subservient to all men in the workplace or place of worship? Can men be so insecure or unfair as to think that God has endowed women with leadership ability just to deny them leadership authority and responsibility? How many men, even pastors, who are adamantly opposed to female clergy honestly think it is fair for women to endure the struggles of educating themselves yet be turned down for promotion solely on the basis of gender? What would they say to their daughters, "The Word of God says . . ."? Can any godly male, in good conscience, contend that the God of the Bible made any human beings sexually, ethnically, culturally, or racially inferior to others? Come on churches . . . can we talk?

In the epistle to Titus, chapter 2, verses 6 through 7, Paul writes to Titus, "Encourage the young men to be self-controlled. In everything set them an example by doing what is good. In your teaching show integrity, seriousness and soundness of speech that cannot be condemned." In this chapter, I have endeavored to emphasize the importance of men in ministering to young women. Once again, I reiterate that the roots that bear the bitter fruit in the lives of young women are watered by their association with the men in their lives, beginning with their fathers. John Maxwell writes in *The 21 Irrefutable Laws of Leadership* that "Leadership is influence, pure and simple, nothing more, nothing less."[2] It has been my experience that deaconesses cannot do what only fathers or father-figures can do. Deaconesses cannot do what only male pastors and male deacons can do. Fathers must be active in the lives of their daughters and model before them the true essence of manhood. Male pastors and male deacons must reinforce God's model of manhood. It is difficult for deaconesses to teach young women what kinds of young men to allow in their lives, especially if their view of manhood is shaped by the streets instead of the church. Why are young women so attracted to the thug image rather than young men who treat them with love and respect? Thugs are all they know! Thugs are their only examples of men. The "B" word and "Ho" are the only references they are comfortable with. Without a father's influence, and the influence of men of character and integrity, African American young women will continue to be attracted to thugs. At least thugs demonstrate integrity and are serious. When thugs say they are going to kick someone's butt, they kick someone's butt. When fathers say they will be over to spend time with their daughters, they may or may not be there. When a pastor or deacon says, "Call me if you need me," young women will most likely listen to voice-mail messages for two weeks. Young women are not that naïve. They are well aware of the pastoral advantages of caller I.D. It stands to reason that young women feel safer with thugs than with fathers who are absent and church men who appear to be weak. I must say that as a woman myself, until I met my husband, I never felt as if I could rely on any male. I never felt completely safe in the company of a male. I have never been involved with a male whom I could use as a standard to measure a husband by. If a deaconess is going to be effective in ministry to young women, she must have examples of and the support of men who are seriously interested in the welfare of women. Otherwise, Madea will still be a more heroic figure than her masculine counterparts, and male rappers will continue to carry more influence than pulpit pontificators.

CHAPTER FOUR
MEETING THE URBAN CHALLENGE—
ORPHANED GIRLS LIVING WITH BOTH PARENTS

"A child left to himself bringeth his mother to shame." (Proverbs 29:15b)

Deaconess Jones & Pastor McCoy

Let's turn our attention to the paradox of the orphan girl who lives at home with both biological parents. We use the designation orphan because this young woman has been allowed to raise herself. Her parents, for the most part, consider they have fulfilled their duties as parents because they have provided the material essentials of life. They haven't a clue that time and discipline are among them. Her room is full of all the up-to-date gadgets and is fit for a princess. It is elaborately decorated with stuffed animals. Barbie and Ken doll collections are only exceeded by posters of Beyoncé, Halle Berry, and Mary J. Blige. Miss Orphan (and sadly, the church) has grown accustomed to her having her own way as she "struts her stuff" wherever she goes, and she goes wherever she gets the whim to go. She wears all the latest brand-name fashions and possesses enough shoes to open her own boutique. She is the first to get the latest multi-colored IPhone. She may be only 15, but she has been wearing too much make up, stockings, and provocative clothing while her parents beam with pride that they are able to give her whatever she desires. They are indeed proud of the fact that her future is secure because tuition for college is already in place. Her parents are totally oblivious to the fact that she has been sexually active since she was 12 years old and has one abortion under her belt. Although she is only 15, she has had at least one same-sex relationship and has been toying with the idea that she may be bi-sexual. The thought is not at all disturbing, as she sees it. In fact, she thinks it adds to her perceived popularity and sensuality and her ability to get attention from both sexes. Although her parents consider her future bright, it is really quite bleak, for by the time she is 18, she will be an emotional wreck. From birth, she has been the apple of her daddy's eye and has been able to wrap him around her little finger. She has won the war with her mother for daddy's affection. Her mother has long since conceded that fact. She can get anything she wants from her daddy by flashing those beautiful brown eyes and saying, "Pleaseee." Sadly, however, nothing she is able to wrangle out of him is enough. She is among the "untouchables" at church, for no one dares discipline her without experiencing the wrath of her daddy, who is a person of power in a position of authority. Even the pastor walks softly in his presence. Therefore, she is allowed to carry herself with a subtle, unspoken social snobbery, above the rules that are applied to her peers.

What's wrong with this picture? Why is she, in reality, a miserable diva? What are her chances of growing into a woman of character? Why is she so scorned by her peers? Could it be because her parents have completely ignored the warnings of Solomon, "Foolishness is bound in the heart of a child" (Proverbs 22:15a), and "A child left to himself will bring his mother to shame" (Proverbs 29:15)? When Solomon said, "bring his mother to shame," "mother" can be viewed as a metaphoric term for God and also the people or parents from which that child descended.

Parents of such orphans have bought into Dr. Spock's modern philosophy of child rearing, allowing their children, especially their daughters, to make major decisions as they relate to selecting friends, male and female, selecting entertainment sources, selecting attire for occasions, and choosing which rules they will obey. Parents allow this freedom because it comes under the law of self-expression. Noted child psychologist Veronica Scott states that "There is nothing more important to childhood development than self-expression. A child must be able to express what he or she wants and how he or she feels with freedom and safety."[1] In our experience, young women who have been raised under such a "modern" approach are more at-risk than young women arriving to the city from Small Town, USA. Whereas the new arrivals are at least partially aware of what they don't know as relates to survival in the city, our Miss Orphan, who has been given too much freedom to express herself, is often more vulnerable because she thinks she knows how to navigate the dangerous waters of the city. She is under the mistaken assumption that she has a good grasp on what goes on in the dangerous world just outside her middle-class, suburban home. This young woman thinks the glitz and glamour of MTV and *Vibe* magazine are "Where it's at," and she is dying to get to it. She has no idea the level of abuse and brutality that awaits her in the shadows of urban America. Therefore, she will put herself in harm's way, thinking that it is the only way to receive what she did not receive at home. The one ray of hope in the life of Miss Orphan is that she must attend church. Although her parents may see church as just an opportunity to flaunt her private piano lessons or voice training, church attendance is actually her only chance to avoid future pain. Her hard-working parents are rightfully proud of her academic prowess and are anxious to embellish how much more advanced their sweet little girl is over the rest of the girls. In reality, however, her parents are living vicariously through the life of a child headed for an emotional train wreck. The church is her only hope. What is the role of deaconesses in such a delicate situation?

Deaconesses' Ministry to "Little Miss Orphans"

First, deaconesses must partner with pastors and other ministry leaders to bring all the associated ministries under the umbrella of a Family Life Ministry. In such a ministry, fathers will learn how to fulfill their roles as fathers, especially in the lives of their daughters. Fathers must be taught that their relationship with their daughter is their daughter's first opposite-sex relationship. It should, therefore, prepare the daughter for every other opposite-sex relationship. In a Family Life Ministry, mothers are taught to be mothers, especially during the early teen years when daughters see them as competition for their father's affection. Mothers must model womanhood in a way that enhances rather than alienates the irreplaceable bond between mother and daughter. In a vibrant Family Life Ministry, daughters are taught their role in the family and their responsibility to contribute rather than to be always on the receiving end. In such a ministry, "me" takes a back seat to "we" as the "we" concept takes control of the steering wheel. In such a scenario, unity is emphasized over independence. In order to achieve the dynamics needed to succeed in the larger society, one must learn the principles of sharing. This principle is vitally important if young women are \to mature into young ladies with character.

The orphan living at home with both parents is often the most difficult of all young women for deaconesses to reach, for she is couched in the bosom of parents who seek to protect her right to flaunt herself, even in the church, in a manner that far exceeds modest apparel. Her parents will often confront anyone who dares confront their daughter with the "rules" that are applied to the rest of the young women at church. Subliminally, her parents have taught her to respond to any attempt on the part of others to correct her with disrespect and behavior unbecoming of a young woman. Young women often boast, "My parents are like my best friends. My mother and I are like sisters. She is my closest confidant. We tell each other everything. We dress alike, and she even allows me to hang out with her when she is with her friends." What a sad scenario! Young women growing up in urban America need parents who have the courage to be parents. Young women have enough so-called friends, enough to fill a stadium. Every young woman needs a father. Fathers, according to Scripture, represent authority in the home. If young women are allowed to manipulate their good ole' daddies to get whatever they desire, where is the authority? Young women need to hear the word "No" as much or more than the word "Yes." Did not God begin His holy list of commandments with "Thou shalt not . . . " (Exodus 20:3)? When daughters hear the word no, it should mean no, and therefore, no barrage of "Please daddies" ought to convert a "No" into a "Yes." Scripture encourages us to "let our yea, be yea, and our nay be nay" (Matthew 5:37). It sets a dangerous precedence when fathers reverse the decisions of virtuous mothers. It is just as injurious for pastors to reverse the decisions of dedicated deaconesses. Fathers and pastors must support the decisions of mothers and mentoring deaconesses.

The most cherished position in the lives of children today, given the emotional absence of so many fathers, is that of a mother. A mother is an invaluable asset. In a culture that preys on young women, perhaps the greatest asset a young woman can be blessed with is a godly mother. Deaconesses and mothers must work harmoniously to ensure the wholesome development of girls into virtuous women. When mothers are resistant to the intervention of devoted deaconesses in the correction of the behavior of their daughters, there are often deeper issues involved. We live in a society where young, African American women are having babies out of wedlock with the motive of receiving the love that was missing in their own lives. Sadly, as a deaconess of over 25 years, I have witnessed many mothers who display a reluctance to discipline their children and will become aggressively defensive when others attempt to do so. In such cases, authority figures such as teachers, policemen, pastors, and deaconesses incur the wrath of mothers in "defense" of their babies. Deaconesses, because they are considered the least of all authority figures, are fed up with getting their hands spanked by persons who should be spanking their children and thanking those who care enough to correct them. We shudder to imagine, however, what will become of our young women if deaconesses do not care enough to correct those attitudes that are sure to bring pain and failure to our future mothers, and hopefully wives (prayerfully, in the reverse order). For few will ever gain the love and respect of men of any great statue without the virtue and moral character that deaconesses can help develop. The ministry of deaconesses in the local church in urban

> *In a culture that preys on young women, perhaps the greatest asset a young woman can be blessed with is a godly mother.*

America is absolutely essential to the future of the African American family.

A Family Life Ministry will bring together all pertinent ministries relevant to developing wholesome group relationships. Sooner or later, youth must learn to respect authority, men must learn to relate to women, singles must understand that they have value outside of a romantic, opposite-sex relationship, and married couples must understand the needs of singles without being threatened by attractive, single men and women.

We believe the greatest benefactor of a Family Life Ministry is Miss Orphan. In such a ministry, she is prepared for the real world. In the real world, the world does not revolve around her. In the real world, rules are non-negotiable, and she will not be able to circumvent them or manipulate men in power by a tearful "Pleaseee." In the real world, her every whim will not be catered to because of the low cut of her blouse or the skimpiness of her skirt. In the real world, she will be exploited for attempting to use her body as legal tender to purchase her own way.

Finally, a Family Life Ministry will prepare Miss Orphan for family life. In such a ministry, she will be exposed to the real price one pays for promiscuity. In her interactions with men without ulterior motives, she will understand how men really view women who cheapen themselves by thinking their bodies are tickets to the top. In her interactions with women, she will learn the skills that teach her to value relationships with other women without the overt or covert cat fights that are so infamous among women. It is imperative for deaconesses to serve as liaisons between Miss Orphan and the world of reality. In the end, however, the greatest step toward saving Miss Orphan from herself is to save her parents from the need to give her everything except themselves. The office of deaconess is one of great responsibility, and to do the work of a deaconess, one must have a calling upon her life.

CHAPTER FIVE
MEETING THE URBAN CHALLENGE—
THE CALLING OF DEACONESSES

"My people are destroyed for the lack of knowledge." (Hosea 4:6a)

Deaconess Jones

We have reached the point in history where the office of deaconess must be recognized as a calling. The work is too challenging, the rewards are too minimal, and the consequences are too critical for the office of deaconess to be conferred upon women simply because they are good and virtuous women. One critical error on the part of a deaconess could mean the difference between life and death. To consecrate a woman to the sacred office of deaconess simply because she is the wife of a deacon would be to ordain a man to the ministry simply because he is a cousin of a pastor. Some wonder why deaconesses are so ineffective in today's church. The simple reason is that there are too many women in the church who wear the hat of a deaconess but who do not possess the *heart* of a deaconess. In the corporate world, I would say the time has come for professional deaconesses. In the church, I must say the time has come for truly anointed deaconesses. Just as professionals in other fields must be prepared through a

> *The office of deaconess must be recognized as a calling.*

strict and disciplined regiment of study and training, deaconesses in the church must be prepared in much the same way, and if one is truly anointed and called by God, the study and training involved will not be loathsome, but embraced.

Such training in one's calling ought to be mandatory because the slightest misdiagnosis could prove disastrous. History gives evidence that the church is notorious for misdiagnosis. During the Inquisition, people who differed with official church dogma were misdiagnosed as heretics and suffered persecution. During the Middle Ages, women whom we now recognize were suffering from PMS (post-menstrual syndrome) were misdiagnosed and labeled by the church as witches and burned at the stake. During the same period, people whom we now know displayed all the classic symptoms of epilepsy were misdiagnosed by the church as demonically possessed and were subjected to exorcisms and execution. Such cases are documented and are now a matter of public record. Such travesties of ignorance continue to this very day. It has been my experience that whatever the church doesn't understand, it credits to the devil. The church, because of ignorance, has given the devil more power than he actually possesses. This kind of unwarranted, unearned, demonic publicity will continue to permit and promote the uncalled, unqualified, gossiping busybodies masquerading as deaconesses who sit in judgment of that which they do not even make an honest effort to understand. If the church is going to ever have an impact in this 21st century, it must take a stand now! If the church is ever going to free itself from the bureaucratic quagmire and complacency that keeps it from making a difference in the lives of our young women, there must be a shake-up in its business-as-usual attitude. The church must be about the mission of seeking and saving the lost, not merely the maintenance of the status quo.

Each time the deaconesses meet in your church, somebody ought to remind them that lives are a stake. I believe God could care less about the kind of flowers that adorn the pulpit. God is more interested in the kind of work we do to save the lives of His children. If we are not reaching out to the children, we are slipping into the caldron of irrelevance. Our children, especially the future mothers of our people, are worth our ignoring the arrogant stares of those who seek to bask in the faded glory of a distant past. The past is but a prologue. It should merely serve as a signpost pointing the way to the future. My daughter would, in all probability, be alive if someone would have taken such a stand a decade ago. It is my passionate obsession that no other mothers will have to endure the pain that I have been forced to endure the past six years. I am committed to making a difference.

For years, my daughter was considered merely a drug addict. Therefore, she was treated as such. She was scorned as being just a "crack-head." The stigma of such a diagnosis caused me to treat her with anger instead of compassion because of my embarrassment. So many ill-informed church leaders, including her mother, lectured down to her and prayed the devil would take his hands off of her instead of embracing her and investigating the true cause of her unexplained drug addiction. It was not until the final few years of her life that

> *The work is too challenging, the rewards are too minimal, and the consequences are too critical for the office of deaconess to be conferred upon women simply because they are good and virtuous women.*

her condition was correctly diagnosed as bipolar depression. When I think of all the years of suffering, all the angry, argumentative confrontations and recriminations, I am aghast and astounded. When I think of the isolation and the suffering in silence that my child had to endure because of the failure of the church and drug treatment specialists to understand the true nature of her illness, I am moved to tears. She, through her self-prescribed medication of cocaine and crack, attempted to find temporary relief from the pain of her illness. Her attempts were futile, and the church's attempts were sincere but damaging to her sense of self-respect. For what the church attempted to extricate through preaching, prayer, and even fasting could have been easily treated through an anti-depressant that was readily available through legal means. What great a price my daughter paid because of the ignorance of church leadership. My daughter was hemorrhaging. My daughter, Sandra, suffered from a very common mental disorder that plagues over 3 million Americans.[1] According to the American Psychiatric Association (APA), 1 in 5 Americans suffer from depression.[2] It was treatable, yet no one recognized what is now so obvious. Drugs are the means by which so many suffering people who do not have quality medical care attempt to cope with their suffering. We blew it. The church failed her. We failed her! The way society condescendingly views people addicted to drugs distracts us from searching for other possible explanations for deviant behavior. The arrogant and condescending way society views people causes us to seek to treat the symptoms by condemning the sufferer. If the bleeding oozes from a physical wound, medical professionals would immediately seek to stop the bleeding, but when a person's soul is bleeding, the church sees no urgency to stop the bleeding but seems rather eager to assign blame. In too many cases, wounded people get salt poured into their wounds as the church takes the archaic view that such wounding is a result of sin, a result of lack of prayer, or a result of one's failure to keep her commitment to God. It is time for the church to emerge out of the Dark Ages and seek enlightenment in treating humanities' diseased souls. After all, the church is the agency that God established on earth to care for the human soul.

How many more of our daughters will have to suffer as a result of the misdiagnosis of uncalled, uneducated, untrained, and uncommitted deaconesses? How many more young women will have to suffer the double-whammy of being victimized and then being blamed by the church for the crimes committed against them? How many more hurting young women who come to the church for help and healing will find themselves injured even more by deaconesses who erroneously assign their injury to a sinful lifestyle, low morals, or a nasty attitude? No other care agency in the world would be allowed to stay in business if it prescribed treatment before conducting a substantial examination. If deaconesses would take time to examine the injured, they would in all likelihood discover that our daughters' wounds are not a result of their own doing. For just a cursory examination of hurting young women would, in many cases, reveal that the culprits of the crime are absent fathers, incestuous relatives, domineering mothers, abusive boyfriends, or sexual predators in positions of authority. It is time our churches stop adding insult to injury and

> *How many more precious, young souls will have to be served the communion elements by deaconesses who are void of the communion attitude?*

begin conducting work on the high plain of decency, sensitivity, and compassion. Too many of our daughters have angrily turned away from the church because the church has recklessly turned against them! How many more precious, young souls will have to be served the communion elements by deaconesses who are void of the communion attitude? How many more of our young girls have to suffer because a deaconess has not been trained to see their needs through their introverted demeanor? How long must pastors be forced to tolerate uncommitted deaconesses who see their position as one of ceremony and not service?

It is imperative, therefore, that the office of deaconess be recognized as a calling because the kind of expertise needed to minister to women day after day calls for a passion that goes beyond minimal duty. After a woman's calling has been recognized and validated through observation, she needs to be trained to conduct her ministry on a level that is at least equal to a level we expect from those who treat our physical infirmities. At the minimum, such training should include instruction in biblical counseling, pastoral care, basic human behavior, intercessory prayer, and ministry to women. Each deaconess should always be in the mode of upgrading her skills and knowledge of her office. Each deaconess should be equipped with a resource manual and encouraged to recommend pastoral consultations and medical evaluations. Those whose calling is to minister to hurting people must be equipped. After initial training, I recommend a period of mentorship under the watchful eye of a seasoned deaconess because the kind of work a deaconess is involved in demands a wisdom that exceeds textbooks.

Additionally, in order for a deaconess to be able to relate to this generation, which is unlike any other generation that has ever lived and has challenges far more complex than the generation of just 40 years ago, deaconesses must spend time learning the current vernacular. Deaconesses should make every effort to be relevant. The problem with most deaconess training material is that it is based upon conducting ministry in a different era than we live in today. It is extremely difficult to minister to young women without an understanding of the language indigenous to their generation. This is not to say that a deaconess should seek to be seen as one of their peers, but surely an effective deaconess must have a general grasp on what is being said. Indeed, one of the most vital assets of a 21st century deaconess in urban America will be her ability to translate the language of the current generation of the inner city. It is in this spirit that I, in a metaphoric sense, set forth the proposition that the 21st century deaconess must have the gift of the "interpretation of tongues."

Spoken language, being the primary means of communication, can be problematic for young women from rural America as they transition to life in the inner city. Words like "dating" and terms like "I love you" often carry a somewhat different meaning in urban America than in Small Town, USA. Such common words and terms may be spelled the same, but if they are not translated accurately, it can lead to major misunderstanding as far as social relationships are concerned. A deaconess that takes her title seriously will seek every edge and make every effort to learn the current linguistic slang and interpret it accurately. Such a well-informed deaconess can save "Miss Country Bumpkin" from bumping her head or from a relationship that breaks her heart. The following is a glossary of contemporary words and terms deaconesses ought to be acquainted with in order to communicate effectively with this generation of young men and women.

Dating

The expression "We're dating" is one that has caused GRITS (Girls Raised in the South) much misunderstanding and grief. When I was growing up in the South, dating was considered going out for an ice cream float, to the movies, or even to a church social. The rural, Southern concept has not changed to any great degree, especially for relatively inexperienced girls raised in the church. When I came to the city of Washington, DC, I had no idea what was expected of me when I was asked out for a date. I had no idea that sex was an expected item on the menu. Imagine my shock when I discovered that dating meant "mating," as with rabbits in heat. I certainly needed an interpreter when I relocated to the city.

Today, the term dating carries with it a variety of meanings depending upon the culture. In some cultures, it denotes casual friendship. In other cultures, it carries the connotation that two people are in an exclusive, committed relationship. In other instances, it may be suggestive of a sexually-intimate relationship. Therefore, deaconesses must encourage young women to remember the admonition of Solomon, "With all thy getting, get understanding" (Proverbs 4:7), prior to accepting dinner.

I Love You

Pastors are often quite adept in pointing out the various words that are translated love from the Greek. Over and over again we hear words like "philo," friendship or brotherly love, "eros," sexual, erotic love, and "agape," unconditional love. These are words translated from the Greek. A deaconess must help young women understand "love" as translated from the street. Love carries regional meanings. As a girl growing up in the ghettos of Charlotte, North Carolina, when I was told by a young man that he loved me, I sincerely thought that he loved *me*: Frances Moore. The person who lived in my body. The girl whom he had gotten to know. The person whom he had spoken with, taken to the movies, and perhaps shared a kiss. Well, that was the definition of "love" in the mind of a love-starved, Southern girl named Frances Moore from Charlotte, North Carolina. I had no idea his language was different than mine. Come to find out, what he loved was the way my naked body felt next to his. I should have known something was different because he only spoke those words before or during intimacy, never afterwards. Hello! But how was I supposed to know? Daddy was gone and mama was silent on the subject.

Today, deaconesses must teach young women the big-city, modern usages of the words "I love you" because in the urban setting, the words "I love you" carry any number of meanings. More often than not, they mean, "I love the size of your breasts and the shape of your legs"; "I love having sex with you"; "I love what you can do for me"; "I love your cooking"; or "I love you for the night."

Imagine a young woman from Small Town, USA who is hungry for love and needing to be needed, and she hears those words from a handsome young man who sings on the choir. Well, as a former naïve, old-fashioned country girl, I have been victimized by the misinterpretation of those words in the city, and I can tell you that they have been a source of great anguish. Oh, how often I wish I would have had someone to interpret those words before I yielded my entire person. If this Southern, country girl had been told the rules of the Northern game called "love," I could have at least been a better player.

Country Girl

With a "country girl," a man from the city automatically tends to feel he has the advantage, and in most cases, he does. The only obstacle that can stand in the way of him having his way is a dedicated, street-wise deaconess. At an alarming rate, while we are sitting in white serving communion on first Sunday morning, country girls are being put under the spell of city boys. Have you ever thought that the country girl is the daughter of Southern parents who are praying night and day that she is under the protective covering of a godly woman? Have we deaconesses ever stopped to think, as we are shouting "Hallelujah" on Sunday mornings, that the country girl is in need of our prayers because she is getting seductive text messages from a smooth-talking city boy? It is time for us to get off our city behinds and make a difference in the lives of thousands of country girls seeking a better life in the cities of our nation.

Making Love

Having sex is not making love. Next question?

Thug

The vast majority of baby boomers are totally ignorant of the contemporary, inner-city meaning of the word "thug." To most church leaders over 50, thug is synonymous to hoodlum, thievish, undesirable. To generation X, the term thug has become the equivalent to manly or soldier, a male that enjoys the admiration of young boys and has rugged traits that appeal to young women in the hood. Consequently, when I would hear well-educated, wholesome young women in the church state they are attracted to young men with a little thug in them, I have been understandably disturbed. Upon further inquiry, I have begun to understand fully why young women make such assertions. Most young women are well aware of the dangers involved with attending social gatherings that include scores of teens and young adults. Therefore, in order to feel secure and protected, the preference of young women is to be in the company of young men who can take care of them in the event "something goes down." Thugs offer such security.

Virgin

Though once a positive, cherished, and lofty characterization to which all young women aspired, today, especially in the inner city, the term "virgin" has become a stigma with which few young women desire to be identified. It is a term that denotes unattractiveness and the inability to get a man. With such a definition in mind, young women, as well as young men, will rarely make such an admission. On the other hand, young men and women who dare claim the virtue of virginity are not virgins in the biblical sense of the word. In the mindset of today's youth culture, those who claim virginity consider it as only the lack of vaginal penetration. In this regard many young people in the church who claim virginity are more active and sexually creative than youth who do not make such claims. In this sexually liberal climate one can participate in oral sex and a variety of exotic sexual activity yet still claim the sexual purity that was once reserved only for people who totally abstained from any form of sexual activity. Up until this generation, the reputation of being a virgin on the part of both young men and young women was a badge of honor. Today, virgin is considered a stigma of naïveté, someone who is a square, socially and sexually inexperienced. With this definition in mind, young men and women who are virgins will rarely make such an admission.

CHAPTER SIX
MEETING THE URBAN CHALLENGE—
THE POWER OF THE TONGUE

"Death and Life are in the power of the tongue" (Proverbs 18:21a)

Deaconess Jones & Pastor McCoy

The one lesson that a deaconess must teach over and over again to every woman within her circle of influence is *the power of the tongue*. No other member of her body carries the kind of power the tongue carries, for good or for evil. Ironically, this is the one lesson that men often master early in life. With the tongue, she can build a successful life or destroy her chances of ever rising above ghetto status. With her tongue, she can reflect the awesome beauty that lies beneath the surface of a rather ordinary appearance, or she can spew forth the ugliness and putrid vomit of a soul polluted

> *With just her tongue, a woman can attract the greatest of men like a magnet or repulse the worst of them like a sick dog with halitosis.*

with anger and bitterness. With just her tongue, a woman can attract the greatest of men like a magnet or repulse the worst of them like a sick dog with halitosis. The tongue can gain a woman access to the offices of power or relegate her to staring angrily at the receptionist until it is time for her to go home. Solomon was right when he said that "death and life are in the power of the tongue" (Proverbs 18:21). Without a doubt, the greatest lesson that any woman can learn is that of *the power of the tongue*. The tongue is the key that opens doors that few men or women can shut.

What is so powerful about the tongue? The tongue's great quality is perception. With the tongue, a woman can give the perception of beauty and respect—even if she has none, love—even if it does not exist, and education—even if she has not spent a day above the fifth grade. Deaconesses ought to encourage young women simply to observe the reactions of people within their field of vision and their responses to women's words. Many women have made these observations and have witnessed the awesome, persuasive power of women who possess control over their tongue. One can see the mastery of the woman who regularly refers to men in a social, or even some business settings, as "honey" and "sweetheart." Most women can see through the mask of women who have been taught how to utilize their tongue to get their way, but few can resist it. Many women look with scorn at the woman who knows how to use words to get her way, but somehow, they do not get the message themselves. However, from sunrise to long after sunset, those women who have learned the lesson of *the power of the tongue* build their own world or destroy the people they love most.

Now it is next to impossible to use words to one's benefit if one is saturated with anger and bitterness. While it is true that many women have good reason to be angry, it is a false assumption for any woman to think she can control her environment in a positive way by using her tongue to demean and tear down loving people. It is true that many African American men struggle with anger, but Solomon reminds the wise woman that "A soft word turns away wrath" (Proverbs 15:1, NKJV). Nothing accents sensuality like the tongue, not a size 8 figure, a push-up bra, or the skimpiest skirt. Nothing makes a man want to come home like anticipating the words "Hey Baby, how was your day?" Nothing endears a secretary to an impatient boss quite like the words, "I'll get right on it, Sir." Nothing sparks friendship with other women, or at least a positive response, like the words, "Girl, that's a beautiful dress" or "That hairstyle on you is fabulous." However, nothing turns people away from a woman like a word spoken with anger or irritation. Most women haven't noticed how the wrong words cause even the kindest people to retreat. Most women do not have the faintest notion how their relationships with the opposite sex are hindered and hampered merely by the way they speak. It is unfortunate that many women do not have the foggiest idea that sweet words make them more attractive than the most stunning dress, the most beautiful hairdo, the most expensive perfume, the most immaculate manicure or pedicure, or even the best cooking. It is astonishing how much time women put into selecting the color for her toe nails or just the right bra from Victoria's Secret and how little time or thought they put into the way they speak to their own husbands. When you study the power Delilah possessed over Samson, the strongest man in the Bible, you

> *Most women haven't noticed how the wrong words cause even the kindest people to retreat.*

clearly see there is no mention of her outward beauty or stunning figure. The one irresistible asset she possessed was the way she used her tongue. Many women pride themselves in "speaking their minds." Little do they realize that to repeatedly "speak one's mind" is to mail your man special delivery and postage paid into the arms of the "strange woman" who "flattereth with her words" (Proverbs 7:5).

Before we leave the issue of the power of the tongue in relationships, we must emphasize the power of the tongue in the corporate world. If Miss Country Bumpkin and Miss Ghetto Mama are ever to rise above their weak economic status to a level above that of a McDonald's counter-girl, they must master the art of English grammar. Time and time again, the deal breaker was bad grammar. One will not even get an interview for the position of receptionist if her grammar is marked by split verbs or what many linguistic experts refer to as Ebonics because the one thing a woman cannot cover up or camouflage is the way she speaks. The moment she opens her mouth, "Oops, there it is!" Bad grammar causes women to be referred to as "bimbos" or "airheads." Deaconesses must equip women to speak life into their lives by speaking well (Proverbs 18:21).

We must also warn women of the negative, intoxicating, seductive power of the tongue, as well. As stated above, if there is one lesson that men have learned well, it is the power of the tongue, as far as women are concerned. It is for this reason that males as young as 13 years old work on their rap. They have witnessed firsthand how females respond to flattery. Miss Country Bumpkin is very vulnerable to the power of a casual compliment from a male. It is for this reason that fathers must take an active role in teaching their daughters the seductive and deceptive ways of insincere, predatory men. The fatherless female is just a compliment away from a painful relationship.

The fatherless female will yield her entire being to the first male who claims he sees her as attractive, intelligent, or irresistible.

One of the most important activities that deaconesses must encourage young women to engage in is listening. As we have stated previously, males learn very early in life the power of the spoken word. With this in mind, young women must be taught the art of listening very early in their development. Young women must be admonished, however, to listen with their heads and not their hearts. The loved-starved heart has gullible ears. Early in any developing friendship/relationship with young men there must be more listening and less kissing. Deaconesses must reiterate over and over again: more listening, less kissing, more listening, less kissing, more listening, **less kissing**! The problem in most relationships is that there was too much kissing (etc.) on the front end. It is a sad, but true, fact that too many young women major in talking and minor in listening.

> *The fatherless female is just a compliment away from a painful relationship.*

Why listen? Because Jesus said, "from the abundance of the heart the mouth speaks" (Matthew 12:34). Attentive listening allows you to sense the heart of the one with whom you are talking and what the person is truly saying. Listening alone will greatly assist young women in discovering what they need to know to make a more accurate determination as to the logical direction in which the relationship should be steered. Listening reveals vital information about the speaker such as his background, values, goals, and spiritual convictions. Young women must be reminded that the Bible is clear when it advises, "be not unequally yoked" (II Corinthians 6:14).

The wise deaconess should teach young women that listening not only includes hearing what men say but, more importantly, also hearing what men *don't* say. Often, what men don't say yields more information than what they say. Young women must be reminded that to withhold the truth is to tell a lie. Therefore, withholding an important truth is telling a dangerous lie. To lie is to claim the devil as one's father, for Jesus said that "our adversary is the father of lies" (John 8:44).

As we bring this chapter to a close, the wise deaconess should help young women learn that the only way they can protect themselves from the negative power of the tongue is to "be swift to hear, slow to speak" (James 1:19). The power of a lying tongue is neutralized by a listening ear.

Deaconess Jones says that the most powerful words she ever heard were spoken by a very attractive young woman. She recalls that the young woman was not in a church but in a subway car. She notes, "I didn't hear what had transpired before or what words preceded her words, but she turned to an extremely handsome and well-dressed young man, cordially smiled, and uttered the five words that gave me hope for young women everywhere: 'No thanks, I'm a Christian.' With that, she exited at the next stop. As she walked away, I became a bit more proud of being a minister."

CHAPTER SEVEN
MEETING THE URBAN CHALLENGE—
SCARY STALKERS AND SAFE HOUSES

"In the time of trouble He shall hide me in his pavilion: in the secret place of his tabernacle shall He hide me." (Psalm 27a)

Deaconess Jones & Pastor McCoy

If a deaconess ministry is serious as relates to its duty to minister to young women, it must set forth the means by which they can be protected. The dangers of the present social and emotional problems of young men are real and often life threatening. At one time, when a relationship did not work out, both parties would agree to go their own way. As we have observed and experienced from over 50 years of ministry between us, to a great degree, absent fathers and angry, and often dominating, mothers have been a driving force as to why young men grow up with serious emotional issues that include intense anger toward women. Such anger has led to an unprecedented rise in emotional abuse and physical violence against young women, in particular. According to the American Institute of Domestic Violence, 5.3 million women are abused each year.[1] Forward thinking deaconesses must be proactive and not merely reactive. They should be aware that sooner or later, a young woman under their watch will be victimized by a stalker. The tragic account of the gasoline attack against Yvette Cade, a beautiful young woman who lived in the suburban

Washington, DC area, is a classic case of stalking. The brutal attack left her permanently scarred. Over and over again, we read newspaper accounts of young men stalking ex-girlfriends and husbands attacking ex-wives. Such men do not accept the prefix "ex," and therefore, feeling fully justified, they inflict great pain upon vulnerable, frightened women. It is time for women to fight back. It is time for women to band together for their own safety and protection. It is time for deaconesses to provide a safe haven for women who are victimized by such dangerous, obsessive, and possessively compulsive men.

Too often, we sit in stunned disbelief and listen to the testimony of young women who have been victimized by such attacks. In tearful and graphic details, they describe how their attackers calmly, and without apparent remorse, carried out their cruel assaults. Time and time again, young women testify they never dreamed their threatening stalker would actually follow through with his threats. Women need to face the fact that if he threatens it, he has thought about it. Too often, what began as cute, flattering jealousy ends in shocking acts of violence. Too often, women tragically miscalculate a man's capacity to inflict pain upon one he professes to love. We wonder, "How could a young man so handsome and astute, with his entire life ahead of him, forfeit it all and become so angry and violent?" Our thoughts: the unnatural absence of fathers has taken its toll on sons. Scripture mourns that "the fathers have eaten sour grapes and their children's teeth are set on edge" (Jeremiah 31:29). It is difficult to fathom such handsome young men with such heinous minds. Why would these young men throw their lives away, simply because a young woman says she needs a little space? Why would a handsome young man, who would have no problem getting to first base with a beautiful young woman, become obsessed to the point that he would douse a woman with gasoline, set her afire, and watch her burn? How could a young, popular college student, with a brilliant career ahead of him, end up maiming or committing cold-blooded murder? Well, the answers are left for psychologists to ponder. The legal penalties are a matter the courts must decide, but the safety of the young, victimized women is, at least in part, an issue that deaconesses must address.

It is unwise for deaconesses to advise women to get out of abusive relationships yet have no place for them to go. It is time for deaconesses to utilize all the means and resources at their disposal to identify emergency housing that can be used by young women as safe havens.

Let us not forget that the writer of Psalm 27 knew what it was like to seek a hiding place from an enraged pursuer. Throughout the Holy Writ we see God using people and places to hide his endangered people. Did not Rahab hide the spies of God (Joshua 2)? Did not Elijah seek a hiding place from Jezebel (I Kings 19)? Did not David hide in a cave from Saul the king, who was determined to kill him (I Samuel 22)? In this spirit, we find David rejoicing as he praises His Lord by singing, "In the time of trouble he shall hide me in his pavilion: in the secret of his tabernacle shall He hide me" (Psalm 27:5). If deaconesses are seriously committed to their calling, they must come together and develop a plan to harbor temporarily young women in harm's way. Many deaconesses have extra bedrooms in their spacious homes. Surely, one of them can be used to save a young woman's life. What a great way to send the message that you truly care! It is our desire that a network of safe houses be set in place throughout the Baptist community in each city. We believe such a network would save countless young women from unnecessary stress and anxiety and unwarranted pain and abuse, not to mention the lives that would be saved.

In addition to shelter, deaconesses ought to have other resources they can draw on for battered women. Deaconesses should keep a resource manual that contains up-to-date information they can reference at a moment's notice. Deaconess meetings are excellent opportunities for emergency drills to ensure deaconesses' readiness for such an emergency. If you have any reluctance in this area, just ask yourself, "What if she were my daughter? Would I want someone to go out of her way for my daughter's safety?" Deaconesses should turn in for the evening with their automobiles full of gasoline, for such crises tend to occur at the most inconvenient hours of the night. Deaconesses must work in tandem with deacons in this regard because a man's presence will certainly provide an additional sense of safety for both the deaconess and the young woman. If deaconesses are not willing to come to the assistance of young women in these circumstances, they should seriously question their calling as deaconesses. The office is not for the faint of heart but rather the spiritually empowered who are ready to act on behalf of the safety of another. Remember the words of the Irish political philosopher Edmund Burke, often quoted by Martin Luther King, Jr., as he admonished the passive majority of good, decent people, "The only thing needed for evil to prosper is for good men to do nothing."[2] The church cannot rely on restraining orders to ensure the safety of young women. How many young women have been murdered or maimed in their own bedrooms with

> *The office [of deaconess] is not for the faint of heart but rather the spiritually empowered who are ready to act on behalf of the safety of another.*

some restraining order on the dresser? The time of deaconess passivity has long since expired. The time for action is at hand. So, deaconesses, begin today. Develop a plan, for evil is sure to raise its ugly head. Paul wrote to Peter, "Be sober and vigilant, because your adversary, the devil, walketh about seeking whom he can devour" (I Peter 5:8). Sometimes it comes down to the childhood game of hide-and-seek. At some point the enemy is going to declare, "Ready or not, here I come!"

As we close this chapter, close your eyes and think of a young woman who is, at this very moment, sitting in her office, walking down the dark street towards her residence, or sitting in her home, frightened out of her wits. She is feeling like a defenseless prey waiting to be devoured. Every unexplained sound increases her terror. She turns the TV up to drown out the scary noises. Then, she quickly turns it down so she can better hear them. She has received several telephone calls, and all she can hear is breathing on the other end. She knows it's him. The last thing she remembers him saying to her was, "It ain't over." It is too late to call someone because it is after 1 a.m. She picks up her Bible to find comfort, but the words are blurred because her hands are shaking uncontrollably. She has never felt the protective hand of a father. The police won't do anything until *he* does something. She prays for morning, yet when morning dawns, she is afraid to leave the house. Where are the deaconesses from her church?

CHAPTER EIGHT
MEETING THE URBAN CHALLENGE—
THE CHURCH, A PLACE WHERE MIRACLES HAPPEN

"Love never fails." (I Corinthians 13:8b)

Pastor McCoy & Nzinga Cardwell

We hear so many horror stories coming out of the church these days that we are often tempted to forget the church is a place where genuine miracles happen. In the Rodgers and Hammerstein, II, Broadway musical *The Flower Drum Song*, there is a tune titled "A Hundred Million Miracles." The most memorable lyric is a line that carries the theme. It says, "A hundred million miracles are happening every day."[1] Nothing could be truer, especially as relates to the African American church in the inner cities of this nation. The church is probably the most criticized institution on earth, yet day after day, year after year, it is the womb that gives birth to many miracles. One of them involves this pastor and a troubled, angry, 14-year-old girl named Nzinga. Nzinga's mother brought her to me out of desperation. Nzinga was acting out in school, being disrespectful to authority, and displaying overall rebellious behavior. Anger was evident in the manner in which she initially communicated with me—total silence. In our first counseling session, as far as she was concerned, I was invisible. She sat in the chair in front of my desk staring at the floor the entire time. As I parried exploratory questions, she seemed to become more agitated. I could see that she, like so many young girls in the inner city, was distrustful of adults whom she thought only pretended to care. At first, as a pastor so inundated with pastoral matters, I truly did not care. In my view, she was just another child acting out. There was nothing wrong with her, I thought, that stronger discipline could not cure. I was as thankful as she that our first session ended. In fact, it was not a session in the proper use of the term but merely a monologue that went on far too long for either of us. The second, third, and fourth sessions went much the same. In fact, I attempted to cancel the final two because I felt nothing productive was taking place. Her mother, on the other hand, felt that progress was being made. I thought, "What progress?" I asked questions, and she responded with silence. The only progress I could see was that she seemed to get more comfortable in that chair in front of my desk.

I cancelled the fifth session by pretending that I had an emergency. I was skeptical when Nzinga's mother said Nzinga seemed angry the session was cancelled. When the fifth session finally commenced, I decided it would be the last since the principle of pastoral counseling is that if progress is not being made within the first three to four sessions, pastors should make a referral to a secular counselor. As a pastor, I am often too busy to spend an inordinate amount of time just in the matter of counseling. With this in mind, I was rather relieved that we were in counseling session number five. By this time, I was more relaxed and less inquisitive. I began to talk about my sons and some of their antics. With that, she seemed to sit up and show some signs of interest. She spotted a photograph of my sons on my desk and asked, "Those your boys?" I was amazed! She actually uttered a sound. I sat in stunned silence. Her response seemed to be, "Don't you know whether or not those are your boys?" I finally got a "Yea" out, and off we were. It was in that fifth session that I was amazed she could actually smile. Such a breakthrough demanded that our sessions continue. During the next few sessions, we began to chat, and I began to see that Nzinga's struggle was with the absence of her father. Such an absence created anger, caused her to act out, and fueled hostility toward anyone who represented authority. As "Zing" began to open up, I actually started to look forward to our sessions. In fact, after that fifth session, our sessions became opportunities for us to share *our* lives. Our "sessions" became daily telephone conversations. If I did not telephone her, she telephoned me. Over the next few years, our relationship grew into a real father-daughter relationship. I began to refer to her as the Princess, and she seemed to bask in that title. She was a rather feisty young woman, getting into fights in school on a regular basis. She seemed to take pride in the fact that her father was coming up to school to talk with the principal. Whenever I would see her at church, I would often teasingly speak by saying, "Zing with the strings of my heart."

    I do not know when the miraculous transitions from pest, to pastor, to parent took place, but I do know that she considers me her father in every sense of the word. Her great frustration was that everyone else did not see me as her father. However, she insists that the miracle of our relationship was the turning point in her life. Subsequently, she graduated from college and is now married and the mother of three boys, the oldest of whom is named in my honor. In addition, she is employed as an academic dean at a Christian academy. Perhaps the crown of our relationship was when I escorted her down the aisle at her wedding.

I believe that what happened between Nzinga and me is a sterling example of the miraculous power of godly love. Paul writes to the church at Corinth concerning its power. In what we know as the "love chapter," Paul states that "love never fails" (I Corinthians 13:8). We are often confronted in today's media with the scandalous behavior of people in ministry. Such an atmosphere has created a perilous paranoia among priests, pastors, and males in positions of authority in the church who seek to reach out to young women who come through the doors of the church. It is well known that those of us in ministry are just an accusation away from scandal and public humiliation. Therefore, most men in ministry are occupying the safe ground of distance. But distance is not what our young people need. If I had taken the safe ground, Nzinga and I would not have a father-daughter relationship today. Sometimes, I shudder when I think of the fact that our relationship almost didn't happen. As in most churches, our developing relationship did not escape the watchful eyes of people looking for impropriety, and it was under such suspicion and gossip that I almost buckled under the pressure to discontinue our communication. It was only through the miraculous capacity of Nzinga to persevere that our relationship became one of the one hundred million miracles that happen every day in the local church. Paul was right when he wrote, "love never fails" (I Corinthians 13:8).

Nzinga's Note

Rarely, if ever, am I asked to reflect upon my relationship with John McCoy, yet privately, I consider the impact daily. When I first met him, he didn't "care" for me because he didn't know me. He only knew what others told him about me. I cannot say I have always had a genuine respect for the man I once thought resembled Martin L. King, Jr., and who embodies a similar life philosophy. What can I write about the man who has become a father to me, the man who changed my life forever? I will begin, I guess, by telling you a bit about me . . . the real Nzinga. As a teenager, I had an ugly temper, a disobedient attitude, and a disrespectful demeanor because I was angry. I was angry that I didn't live in a home with a mother and father present which, in my mind, meant I would not have the same experiences and opportunities that many of my friends would have. While my mother did her best to keep me in private school and expose me to sports, arts, and culture, there was still a void! That void was manifested as the "father-wound," or absence of a father, which, in my opinion, is one of the deepest, most hurtful, and discouraging voids a girl can suffer. To me, the absence of a male presence in my home was suffocating! When I first met John McCoy, I couldn't breathe! I was drowning in my own blood, choking on my own saliva, dying in a pool of self-hatred.

    I remember walking into his office not knowing what to expect but excited that my mother had asked her pastor to talk to me about my behavior and my poor attitude. Oh, and my failing grades! I don't know what I thought was going to occur, but I had no idea this pastor had maybe missed his life's calling. And by that, I mean he was working as a pastor but should have changed the sign on his office door to indicate that he was a PSYCHOLOGIST! By the time we finished our first meeting, I was in tears and had realized that I was not as tough as I thought! I answered him with one word, no matter the question, all the while thinking, "I'm going to tell him what I think he wants to hear so we can talk about what I want to talk about!" Well, that worked until he asked me about my father. As soon as he did, the tears began to stream down my face. All he asked was, "Where is your father?" Even today, at 34, I can remember the strong emotion and sting that I felt, the lump in my throat, and the anxiety in my stomach. I was in *physical pain! As much as I tried, I couldn't control or stop the tears from falling. "How embarrassing is this?" I thought. "Now this man knows where I am weak!" Needless to say, that meeting came to an abrupt end, and we decided we would talk again soon. I was so glad to get out of that office, and I know he was glad to get me out! Even though that meeting was a disaster, we were obligated to talk again. In the meetings that followed, God cultivated our relationship and began the process of shaping us into father and daughter.*

The strange thing is that neither of us set out to have a relationship that was more than a "pastor-parishioner" connection, but God knew. The more time we spent together, the more I began to understand the complex emotions that were carrying me from happiness to frustration and anger on a regular basis. I also began to discover my true potential for greatness. I took pleasure in the fact that he called me every morning to make sure I was up on time for school, and he called my mother to make sure my behavior was improving. Even if I only made small steps, I knew he cared. I respected him because he cared enough to be consistent, and there was fidelity. He was committed to me, dedicated to making sure that I was successful in all of my endeavors. I cannot recall the countless hours we spent on the telephone or riding in the car just talking. I told him everything about me, and he listened to the things that were important to me. We talked about boys, history, life, work, traveling, current events, the future, and everything in between. I knew what he was going to say before he said it, and he knew what I was going to say before I said it. We can still do that today! We smile at one another because we almost know exactly how the other will respond in awkward situations. Often times, after we have experienced a tense moment, we will come together and explode into laughter recounting the most embarrassing, yet hilarious, moments. Because he is a pastor and president of a school, he encounters many people who know him, but he doesn't remember their names. Whenever we are out, without a doubt, we will run into someone who rushes toward him with all the excitement and passion of a best friend of 40 years, and as the person is approaching, I will gently whisper his or her name so he is not totally at a loss. When the person leaves, he will say, "Whewww, thanks!" And of course, we laugh!

While I don't have enough time or space (after all, this is not my book) to share with you in depth, I pray that through my brief note you are able to understand just how this relationship has impacted my life. John McCoy saved my life, before I even met him. I didn't think I was of any value. I knew that my mother loved me and that my grandparents loved me, but beyond that, I felt alone, like no one understood me. I thank God daily for this father-daughter relationship because God knew what I needed. While I have not fully healed from the "father-wound," I have made a great deal of progress. I am not as angry as I used to be because I realize that if my biological father had not been absent, John McCoy could not have been present! I have likened my life before to the hymn, "Love Lifted Me" by James Rowe.[2] The first verse, in particular, "I was sinking deep in sin, far from the peaceful shore / very deeply stained within, sinking to rise no more / but the Master of the sea, heard my despairing cry / and from the waters lifted me, now safe am I . . . Love lifted me . . . when nothing else could help (not punishment, or spankings, yelling, or screaming) / love lifted me!" I cannot end this note without thanking my mother for trusting her pastor enough to mentor me and shepherd my heart. She was self-less and self-sacrificing because she wanted more for me. With all the sociopaths in our society, including sometimes in the church, my mother could have thought twice about releasing me to her pastor. She could have cut the *relationship off at any time, but instead, she trusted God and applauded the change in behavior. She supported us wholeheartedly, never wavering because she knew that the love was pure and a beautiful reflection of our Savior's grace. My mom can soften my heart when I am angry by using my dad. She simply says, "Zing, Pastor has been good to you." Immediately, my anger dissipates because he has, in fact, been good to me. God used him to change my life!*

****

Such is one of the "hundred million miracles" that occur in the African American church every day as we reach out to young women. It is my hope that women like Fran Jones will, to use the well-known metaphor from Martin L. King, Jr.'s, August 28, 1963 *I Have a Dream* speech, hue out of their mountains of despair stones of hope as they seek to minister to the hurting women in our society. These women have nowhere else to turn. They are lost on lonely islands of pain, anger, distrust, and unforgiveness.

Somewhere between their pain and anguish there needs to emerge a deaconess who cares enough to go beyond the traditional job description. There is a saying that defines tradition as "where God used to be." Truer words have never been spoken. God used to be held up within the four walls of the church. God used to be in the judgment business. God used to be in the ceremonial ritualism that the church is so known for. God used to be in the business of separating the sheep from the goat, with no regard as to how or why "goats" became "goats." But wait! Are these places where God used to be or where churches that were engulfed in spiritual ignorance used to be? Today, I see God in the miracle of deaconesses who care enough to be concerned about women who have babies out of wedlock. I see God in deaconesses who embrace young girls without daddies. I see God providing a safe haven for abused and frightened women who have nowhere else to turn. I see God in deaconesses as they remember what it was like to be young and foolish, in need of love, and making all the wrong decisions. Finally, I see God in deaconesses as they care enough to purchase church dresses for young, urban girls who have never been to church. I see God at work as those deaconesses pick up these young women for church. So deaconesses, where do you desire to be? In ignorance, where it was thought God used to be or in reality, where He has always been and thus, where He is today and forever (Hebrews 13:8)? Someone once said that "Compassion is the mother of miracles."[3] Deaconesses, when was the last time God used you to give birth to a miracle? Remember, the black church, especially, is a place where a hundred million miracles happen every day. Miracles happen where deaconesses care. It is my sincere belief that the God who uses the church to give birth to one hundred million or more miracles every day desires to perform many such miracles in the lives of the young, naïve African American women most at risk.

CHAPTER NINE
MEETING THE URBAN CHALLENGE—
THE YOUNG WOMEN MOST AT RISK

"Behold, I send you forth as sheep in the midst of wolves: be ye therefore wise as serpents, and harmless as doves. Beware of men" (Matthew 10:16 & 17a)

"That they may [the aged women] teach the young women to be sober, to love their husbands" (Titus 2:4)

Pastor McCoy

As a pastor of an inner city church, the metaphor of sheep and shepherd has become very important to me. Sheep are some of the most defenseless of all creatures. Sheep have no physical defenses against wolves. Yet, in the urban areas of these United States, sheep are "in the midst of ravenous wolves." The great hope of sheep then, according to our Lord, is the mind. In Matthew 10:16, sheep are advised to be "wise as serpents." Wisdom, the byproduct of knowledge, is the best weapon in the very limited arsenal of sheep.

My greatest concern for young women in the urban battlefields of our country is education. I use the word "battlefield" because young women not only find themselves as unwitting combatants with predatory males who lurk in crowded city streets, bustling stations, and dark corridors, but they also battle for the prize of a husband—and like it or not, the competition is steep in the city. As I have conducted ministry, especially among African American women, it has been my experience that they dislike my use of the word "competition," but let's be real, the struggle for the attention of the few good men who inhabit the urban areas of our cities is just that—a competition. Time and time again, as I speak to single, African American women, I hear their pessimism as relates to finding a suitable mate among African American men. In a November 2003 *Ebony* article, Joy Bennett-Kinnon notes that the percentage of Black women who are married declined from 62 percent to 31 percent between 1950 and 2002. She suggests that an increasing number of Black women will never get married. Though the reasons vary, the primary reason that African American women cite that I have spoken with is the dearth of decent, available, educated African American men. This scarcity can be attributed to lack of education, war, incarceration, and homosexuality, among other issues. The lack of young, eligible, potential husbands can be seen on any given Sunday in a local church. Therefore, moral young men have a great advantage when it comes to selecting a wife. The Word says, "whoso findeth a wife, findeth a good thing" (Proverbs 18:22a). I would also add, a plentiful thing. So, as a young woman's biological clock continues to tick away her child-bearing years, what's a young woman to do? How can a young woman increase the value of her stock?

There are many variables that make a young woman special. There is a certain something that makes a young man see a particular young woman as the one you take home to Mama. Deaconesses must advise young women in this area above all others because the physical training and cosmetic industries are making a mint on selling to young women that outward beauty will increase their chances to land "Mr. Right." While physical beauty will certainly get young men's attention, I am sure that young women who possess physical beauty are tired of merely getting the attention of young men. I am reasonably certain that young, outwardly attractive women have had their fill of "dead-end dates" or dates where the ultimate goal in the mind of men is the bedroom instead of the church altar. Though men are intrigued and initially stimulated by outward beauty, for the most part, we are looking for more than a trophy wife. In fact, men are egotistically insulted when women think men are so shallow that all it takes to attract them is outward attractiveness. Perhaps the saddest observation that I, as a pastor in the inner city, have made is that young women spend too much of their time thinking that outward beauty is the answer to their loneliness. Imagine the insecurity of winning the love of a man by outward attractiveness. Outward attractiveness is fleeting and subject to health, age, and the vicissitudes of life. Deaconesses must assist pastors in teaching the truth that will free young women from such a futile approach to companionship.

It is with this erroneous approach to the issue of men in mind that I encourage deaconesses to help young women see the importance of "adorning themselves in modest apparel" (I Timothy 2:9). As the bodies of young women begin to develop, they begin to get an idea of the power of sexuality. Even in the church, they are aware that men who previously saw them as children begin to see them as women. Young women

> *Deaconesses must assist pastors in teaching the truth that will free young women from such a futile approach to companionship.*

become conscious of the subtle "sneak peeks" of even older men in the church. The power of bulging breasts and crossed legs opens up a new world previously unknown to young women who were once tomboyish. It is then that young women decide that being sexy gets attention. Thus, sexiness becomes the ultimate lure, alchemy, a ticket to the much-desired realm of attention. The wise deaconess, however, must begin to teach young women what many young, immature mothers fail to teach them which is the power of modest apparel. Though men are intrigued by what they see, they are mystified by what they do not see. A young woman must be taught that dressing too revealing is to cheapen and devalue herself. Modest or conservative apparel will heighten how she is viewed.

Deaconesses must also teach young women that promiscuity is not the answer. The more promiscuous a young woman becomes, the more her opportunities for marriage diminish. The line "I'll love you more afterwards" is one of the biggest lies the Adversary has ever regurgitated. Most men that I have talked with are adamant that a woman with a reputation for being promiscuous commands less respect from a man. The people most responsible for teaching young women the value of morality are their parents. Too often, however, by the time young women understand the value of morality, they have already lost their virginity. But thankfully, God has provided an answer to such a dilemma, and it is called "regeneration." This feature of Christianity stands head and shoulders above all other religious faiths. The chance for a new beginning, a rebirth, is what the grace provided by the sacrifice of Jesus Christ offers. To be "born again" (John 3) is an opportunity for what is popularly called "second virginity."[1] It is the spiritual opportunity of a lifetime.

It is the answer to increasing the possibilities of marital bliss. It can increase a woman's chances of landing Mr. Right and maintaining his interest for a lifetime. The unmerited favor wrought by the Christian faith begins the building of character. There is no substitute for character. Character is the greatest attribute of a good woman. Character produces the attitude that draws good men. Character is developed slowly as a young woman grows in a wholesome environment. Character is a result of the investment of caring parents. Character is a by-product of the love of a father and the model of a loving, virtuous mother. Character is what sways the pendulum in the direction of a godly woman and away from the fine woman with the attitude. This is not to say that there are no attractive women without attitudes in the church, but the presence of physical beauty early in life often dissuades a woman from the necessity of developing character. Young women who were not born with an overabundance of outward beauty often develop other, more important, aspects of their person.

The ministering deaconess can facilitate character building by helping young, African American women redirect their anger. As I facilitate the men's Bible class at the church where I serve as senior pastor, overwhelmingly, the men (whose ages range from 16 to 80) contend that nothing is more unattractive to African American men than an angry woman. African American women have endured and overcome while being victims of abuse, being sexually exploited, and being discriminated against because of gender by men in general as well as by men in the church. African American women are also the most frequent targets of African American male aggression. Even with these weights on their backs, our young women must be taught how not to allow anger to define neither who they are nor undermine their destiny. Under the caring and compassionate ministry of deaconesses, young women can, with the power of the Holy Spirit, have their anger transformed and channeled into a passion to succeed and serve God to a level heretofore unknown. The tremendous energy that is generated by anger can indeed be transformed into a powerful force that can propel young women to heights beyond their wildest dreams.

Deaconesses, however, must possess the wisdom to minister to young women in a way that suggests and feels like love and not control or manipulation. According to several focus groups I have led, both men and women become extremely angry when they feel they have been manipulated. Therefore, I believe that pastors, teachers, and deaconesses must teach young women that manipulation, once discovered, will destroy a relationship. (I know that it may appear that most of my criticism is directed toward women, but this publication's focus is on how deaconesses can help young, African American women. If I were addressing the issues of African American men, I would speak just as strongly, or even more so because I believe that we men have more issues in regards to manipulation than women.) Young women are often perplexed by men's propensity to keep their thoughts and emotions to themselves. But make no mistake about it, men are extremely perceptive creatures. Men are very observant when it comes to the games that some women play. Men are extremely conscious of some women's manipulative efforts to control their environment and exposure to other women. Men are extremely aware of the distrust that some women have for them and other women whom they deem more attractive. Men are also aware of some women's need to control, and most men allow such control without much protest. The problem, however, is that an effort to control through manipulation does not generate more love or trust in men for women. Manipulation, in any form, creates an atmosphere of suspicion and distrust. For African American men, in particular, the perceived effort on behalf of African American women to control them stirs up two emotions. First, it is painfully reminiscent of the control white America has exerted upon black men. Secondly, such perceived control on the part of a man's mate creates resentment in that it is insulting to his intelligence and a manipulation of his fragile ego. Devious women are not nearly as attractive to men as women who have no guile. Nothing turns the African American man off, or towards other women, quite like feeling controlled and manipulated.

It is imperative also for deaconesses to emphasize the importance of education to young women. I have witnessed the frustration of too many young, African American women in the area of education. The difficulty on the part of African American men to economically succeed in America has caused them to look for a real helpmeet. I am amazed at women who, for whatever reason, harbor resentment toward well-educated young women. Such resentment is often played out in churches, as church is a place where people of diverse backgrounds convene. Instead of sulking, having a crisis of self-esteem, harboring resentment because of unfulfilled goals, or frustrating their men to the point they are pushed into the direction of a more educated woman, young women should become determined to get the education it takes to create a brighter future. The opportunities are limitless for well-educated women, and there are many creative and innovative means by which to finance such education.

As I have talked with young, African American women, I have found that there are many who abhor or detest the word "compete," especially as it relates to gaining the attention and affection of a spouse. I hear women say, "I shouldn't have to compete or be compared." The truth of the matter is, whether one likes it or not, a competition for the most compatible partner exists, and it seems to be an innate part of human nature to compare. And in such a materialistic culture as American society, competition exists in areas in which most people think it ought not to exist. Even on the pastoral level, we pastors are fully aware that we are constantly being compared as we observe the game of musical chairs that church goers play from Sunday to Sunday. Pastors, like many women, are resentful that after all we do for members of our congregations, many members move from church to church simply because in their minds the new pastor preaches "better" than the one who has stood by their families through many turbulent storms. Ideally,

> *A determined young woman and a dedicated, resourceful deaconess is an unbeatable combination.*

such should not be the case, but we don't live in an ideal world. The commercial industry constantly feeds the competitive hunger of human beings to be in a constant mode of playing the field, always searching for that which is "new and improved." Wives search for the best product, and many husbands, subconsciously, search for a better wife. I am convinced that the better wife can be his present wife if she is in a continual mode of self-improvement. In today's society, fewer and fewer people are in the business of settling. If a woman is not happy and it does not appear her partner is truly concerned about improving her level of happiness, then this throw-away culture has no problem with the "out with the old, in with the new" attitude that has created a disaster for family life. It is in this spirit that deaconesses must begin to focus on those young, African

American women furthest from the top, as far as education is concerned.

In today's economy, young men are convinced that they will not contend with the anger, manipulation, and lack of education for which many African American women are so noted. I believe that with the proper encouragement, single young women raised in poverty, even if they are mothers with dead-beat dads, can rise to positions of strength with determination and the help of dedicated deaconesses. Deaconesses must first encourage them not to waste another second complaining about dealing with baby-daddy drama or about what they don't have. I believe that a determined young woman and a dedicated, resourceful deaconess is an unbeatable combination. The work of the deaconess is critical for those who are raising the next generation. Young women can know success, happiness, and what it is like to have meaningful relationships. Young, single women with children can rise to heights beyond their wildest dreams if deaconesses are serious about their work. Fran Jones, in her book *The Making of a Deaconess* (2000),[2] marvels at how differently her early life would have been were there just one deaconess who cared enough to look beyond her swollen belly and see her hurting heart. Deaconesses, it is a much better approach to light a candle rather than curse the darkness. Deaconesses, strike your matches and create the incentive spark that fires up young women to return to school to attain an education, not only to gain the interest of suitable, potential male partners but also to compete in an ever-expanding job market. Too many young African Americans who are mothers wait in vain for the fathers of their children to do the right thing. Meanwhile, the futures of their children are getting dimmer and dimmer. Deaconesses must work with a fervent, obsessive urgency to break the pathetic cycle of poverty among young, African American women.

When the topic of higher education is raised in the inner city, the quintessential question of funding is raised, not only for tuition but also child care. As a pastor, I am amazed at the extent to which young women and men misuse their financial resources. Funds are spent on ear piercings, naval piercings, tongue piercings, tattoos, manicures, pedicures, cosmetics, and hair extensions—not only for mothers but for infants and young children, as well. Yet, when it comes to getting the most valuable commodity of an education, young people are stumped as to how it can be financed. There are many programs especially designed to assist young mothers with their educational pursuits. Community colleges are a valuable resource, and they offer an alternative to the traditional, four-year academic pursuit. The church can assist with information and resources needed to facilitate such an endeavor. The church can also aid with child care. Where there is a will, there is a way. First, however, there must be a will.

A good education can open many doors. An education expands an individual's world and broadens her horizon. The world looks differently through the eyes of education. Education adds a dimension to a woman's character that makes her more interesting. Physical attraction may get a man's initial attention, but an education will add a dynamic to the conversation that will help to keep it. Without an education, a young woman commits social suicide the moment she opens her mouth. Without education, a dining experience will reveal her lack of basic etiquette. In certain social circles, an education will allow her to laugh with instead of being laughed at. It always amazes me how young women desire men in the corporate arena but do not possess the basic social graces to be an asset to such men.

The well-read, well-informed wife can be the deciding factor as to whether or not he lands that important corporate position. On the other hand, a gum-chewing, verb-splitting, mouth-full-of-food-talking wife can be a deadly liability to a man on the way up. The Bible's admonition to "be not unequally yoked" (II Corinthians 6:14) carries a much deeper meaning than mere religious compatibility. Often, the only reliable and loyal partner a man of status or lofty position has is his vigilant and educated wife.

Finally, deaconess must teach young women to minister to men. Perhaps the most significant intangible that a young woman who desires to increase her chances of marriage must possess is the ability to help a man de-stress. Women must seek to be the solution to the stress of men rather than the source. Highly successful men are those who spend an enormous amount of time honing their craft. Such time is why they are successful. A man is fully aware that there is a fine line between success and failure. He is also aware that while he is spending an excessive amount of time with a needy or high maintenance woman, his competition is moving forward. Great success is a result of great sacrifice on the part of many people. Successful men are often extremely tunnel-visioned. They possess the ability to focus totally on a certain project for a long time, to the exclusion of everything and everyone around them. Such men are often temperamental, which is a result of a giftedness that causes them to be impatient with the ordinary and mundane, but necessary, issues of life. They find it very difficult to establish balance in their lives. It is for this reason that it is to a man's benefit that he does not marry, or at least not marry and have children, until he can spend ample time with his family. However, such is not always the case. What if President Obama would have waited until he became president before he married? He would never have become president. To a larger extent, First Lady Obama was blessed with the ability to truly be a helpmeet for the president of the United States. Such ability is not by osmosis or accident. It is a direct result of education, nurturing, and wise counsel, the same kind of wise counsel that deaconesses must convey to future corporate wives and first ladies. Young women must develop the discipline to know that when successful men come up for air, they need to exhale. He will turn toward the woman who can best assist in that exhaling.

With this in mind, young women need to cultivate the ability to give him what he needs. A sense of humor, an interest in his work, a suggestion that triggers a thought, an understanding tone. Even the ability to allow him time to himself will create an unbreakable bond between a man and a woman. Young women must understand that a man's work is a great part of his life, and therefore, when a relationship with a woman becomes too much work, guess which job gets the letter of resignation. Young women should be taught to become a part of a man's work. With this in mind, young women should be well read as relates to any area of his work. To win a man's heart is to be not only interested in him but to be also interested in what interests him. Enthusiasm and excitement toward his work and play are the glue that keeps a woman by her husband's side as a partner rather than on the side lines as an uninvolved observer.

There are certain intangibles that cause a man seeking to be successful to select a particular young woman over the millions of others as a lifetime partner, and the aforementioned are just a few. Therefore, to the ultimate question, "What would cause a man seeking to be successful in life to select a certain young woman as his lifelong mate among the millions of women in the world?" There are no simple answers. However, the vast majority of young men striving for success that I have posed this question to almost overwhelmingly stated that the young woman must possess an ambition compatible to his, accompanied by a zeal, zest, and contagious enthusiasm for life that supersedes most. In addition, the young woman who desires to stand out from the throngs of other young women raised in the inner city must possess a rock-hard determination to rise above her meager surroundings and reach for a level of living that separates her from her competing peers.

In this chapter, I have emphasized success. Depending on the individual, the word success carries different meanings. It is imperative that a potential husband and wife team has a clear understanding of the definition in their relationship. Success, to men, usually means establishing a career that brings fulfillment, while for women, success may mean developing a fulfilling relationship. Without first defining success, becoming successful will be illusive at best. In order for a collective success to be achieved, each party must embrace the other person's definition of success. She must do all within her power to be his helpmeet, and he must do all within his power to fulfill her need, too, for a relationship on which she can depend. Deaconesses must encourage young women not to settle for the sake of a wedding ring. Wedding rings are symbolic of the endless, mutual love and respect two people share with each other, not one party's endless, unilateral effort to get his or her own way.

As we close this chapter, I must emphasize that, without Christ, and the wisdom of a wise, godly woman, it is next to impossible for a young woman to make the transition from a stereotypical uneducated "ghetto mama" into an elegant and interesting lady that a godly and ambitious young man is in search of as a life partner. There is an old saying, "You can't make a silk purse out of a sow's ear." To put it harshly, "You can't make a lady out of a tramp." Some contend that Broadway musicals are only the stuff that dreams are made of, merely a figment of a writer's imagination. No man can take an Eliza Doolittle and pass her off as a dignified lady of culture, despite how well she is able to repeat, "The rain in Spain stays mainly in the plain." While it may be true that a young woman's painful or abusive past can emboss indelible scars of anger in her heart toward men, it may also be true that some African American women, because of the dysfunctional environment in which they were raised, often harbor resentment toward other women and disrespect toward anyone who seeks to lead them out of the darkness of their familiar surroundings into the bright light of a future filled with limitless possibilities. However, I believe that the redemptive the love of Christ can make a marvelous difference. I have been the pastor of a church in the inner city of Washington, DC for over 26 years, and I am a witness that through Christ, "a hundred million miracles happen every day."[1] I have seen the power of Christ transform anger into peace of mind, despair into hope, and indifference into determination to pay the high price to succeed. The key in most cases was a human being who truly cared—a human being who matched one's indifference with a determination to make a difference in one's life. Every day when I drive through the streets of the inner city and see young women who have never been given the inspiration to succeed, I see the need for deaconesses. Every time I stand in a fast food line waiting my turn to be served, I witness young women either behind the counter or in front of it whose lives are severely limited by the ambivalence of deaconesses. Every time I hear young women refer to each other as the "B" word, with hands on their swiveling hips giving someone a piece of their minds, I silently pray that deaconesses grasp the great need to reach out and embrace these young women at risk. The alternative is too horrendous to fathom.

They are the mothers of the next generation—and surely, the hands that rock the cradle are the hands that shape the 21st century.

AFTERWORD
Pastor John L. McCoy, D. Min.

"In the time of trouble He shall hide me in his pavilion: in the secret place of his tabernacle shall He hide me." (Psalm 27a)

As the pastor of Fran Jones for over a quarter of a century, I want to conclude this book by congratulating her for her sincere desire to help hurting young women. Fran Jones is the epitome of what it means to bear the title of deaconess. I say "bear" and not "wear" because to be a deaconess is to bear a burden for those who are hurting. Deaconesses must move beyond the communion table into the community. This new century has brought with it a plethora of problems. The level of such problems is unprecedented in the annals of human history. While it is true that the 20th century witnessed great strides being made on behalf of the liberation of women, the stress accompanied with such strides has created a backlash of anger toward women. Many African American men are uncomfortable, angry, and insecure because of the upward mobility and independence of African American women. Sadly, the church, in many cases, has been the principle culprit in this animosity toward women. Erroneous teachings concerning male and female relationships have fanned flames of male anger and insecurity. The church's emphasis on biblical passages such as "let the women learn keeping silence with all subjection" (I Timothy 2:11) has continued to silence the church on matters concerning the basic rights of women. Our churches cannot empower African American men by silencing African American women. It is, therefore, incumbent upon our churches to do all within our power to reverse the damaging dogma that has been inflicted in ignorance. The necessary reversal is next to impossible through Sunday morning male preaching alone. It is in this regard that the work of deaconesses like Fran Jones is essential and irreplaceable.

Fran Jones is a survivor. My wife and I were present the night Fran was forced to deal with the pain of her daughter's murder. No mother should ever have to experience what Fran experienced on that night. Since that night, Fran and I have engaged in many conversations about how to prevent such tragedies from being visited upon other mothers. We have come to the conclusion that there are no quick or easy fixes to the issues that bring about such catastrophic occurrences. One of the necessary, inescapable approaches to preventing such tragedies is a corresponding ministry for men. Deaconess Jones and my combined 50 years of ministry to African American women and men give witness to the fact that an overwhelming cause of the pain and degradation of African American women is African American men. And when we say men, we are not only referring to uneducated, angry young men that we can find on any street corner in urban cities. When we set forth the premise that one of the major causes of the pain of African American women is men, we are referring to pastors, deacons, and all men of influence who in one way or another demean women.

If the church of the critical decade ahead is going to remain relevant, it must begin to reconsider its biased teachings designed to reinforce the supremacy of men. These times call for a new paradigm of men's ministry, which includes men, often for the first time, listening to women. How can we men, especially those of us who preach to congregations that include up to 80% women each Sunday, begin to heal women if we do not hear women? Therefore, women must not be admonished to be "silent in the church" but encouraged to speak up and speak out in the church. As painful as it may be, those of us men who bear the responsibility of healing families must be willing to truly listen. Women like Fran Jones have gained a wealth of wisdom that could truly empower both African American men and women. It will be then, and only then, that males and females will become as our Creator has designed, companions and not competitors.

The ministry of Fran Jones represents hope: hope for the millions of young, African American women the church has failed. Hope for the countless young women who sit silently in the church, or quietly in some doctor's office, wondering about their futures. Hope for the young, African American woman who is sitting on the edge of her bed at this very moment with a handful of sleeping pills, wondering if life is worth living. The 21st century will challenge the church in a way that it has never been challenged before. It will finally force the church to deal with issues affecting women. If women are ever to be seen as more than objects of male gratification who should just "keep their mouths shut" and suffer in silence, the church must respond to the challenge. Such is the challenge of our day. Fran Jones seeks to respond to the challenge!

NOTES

Introduction: Meeting the Urban Challenge

1. Donald A. McGavran, *Understanding Church Growth* (Grand Rapids: Eerdmans, 1970), 278.
2. Joe Young and Sam M. Lewis, "How Ya Gonna Keep 'Em Down On the Farm After They've Seen Paree" (New York: Waterson, Berlin & Snyder Co., Music Publishing, 1919)
3. Paul Laurence Dunbar, "Life," lines 1-4, Poetry X, accessed September 27, 2004, http://poetry.poetryx.com/poems/6224.

Chapter One: A Deaconess Birthed by Pain

1. Brett and Kate McKay, "Manvotional #5: 'Invictus' by William Ernest Henley," The Art of Manliness, last modified October 5, 2008, http://artofmanliness.com/2008/10/05/manvotional-5-invictus-by-william-ernest-henley/.

Chapter Three: Meeting the Urban Challenge—Not for Deaconesses Only

1. Sam Husseini, "Martin Luther King Jr: 'Why I am Opposed to the War in Vietnam,'" last modified January 10, 2007, http://www.husseini.org/2007/01/martin-luther-king-jr-why-i-am.html.
2. John Maxwell, *The 21 Irrefutable Laws of Leadership: Follow Them and People Will Follow You,* (Nashville: Thomas Nelson, 1998), 11.

Chapter Four: Meeting the Urban Challenge—Orphaned Girls Living with both Parents

1. Veronica Scott, "Children and Self-Expression," Article City, http://www.articlecity.com/articles/parenting/article_1626.shtml

Chapter Five: Meeting the Urban Challenge—The Calling of Deaconesses

[1] "Bipoloar Disorder," MSN, http://health.msn.com/health-topics/bipolar-disorder/bipolar-disorder-5.
[2] Alice Drinkworth, "Depression About Being Single," Ehow Family, http://www.ehow.com/about_6790155_depression-being-single.html.

Chapter Seven: Meeting the Urban Challenge—Scary Stalkers and Safe Houses

[1] Jane Powell, "Domestic Violence (Physical and Emotional Abuse): Questions to Ask," Meditations for Women, http://www.meditationsforwomen.com/articles/Article/Domestic-Violence--Physical-and-Emotional-Abuse----Questions-to-Ask/66.
[2] "Edmund Burke Quotes," http://thinkexist.com/quotation/the_only_thing_necessary_for_the_triumph_of_evil/158330.html.

Chapter Eight: Meeting the Urban Challenge—the Church, a Place Where Miracles Happen

[1] "Memorable Quotes for Flower Drum Song (1961)," http://www.imdb.com/title/tt0054885/quotes.
[2] "Love Lifted Me," last modified October 11, 2007, http://www.cyberhymnal.org/htm/l/l/lliftdme.htm.
[3] "Bishop T.D. Jakes Sermons on Healing," last modified Februray 24, 2009, http://christonline.wordpress.com/2009/02/21/bishop-td-jakes-sermons-on-healing/.

Chapter Nine: Meeting the Urban Challenge—The Young Women Most At Risk

[1] Shannon Primicerio, "Can I Still be Pure if I've Already Lost My

Virginity?" last modified July 21, 2009, http://beingagirlbooks.com/blog/2009/07/can-i-still-be-pure-if-ive-already-lost-my-virginity/.

[2] Fran A. Jones, *The Making of a Deaconess* (Jonesboro, AR: Four-G Publishers, 2000), 24.

[1] "Memorable Quotes for Flower Drum Song (1961)," http://www.imdb.com/title/tt0054885/quotes.

Proof

Made in the USA
Charleston, SC
28 July 2011